The
Runner's
Field
Manual

The
Runner's
Field
Manual

A Tactical (and Practical) Survival Guide

Mark Remy
and the Editors of RUNNER'S WORLD®

RODALE

© 2010 by Rodale Inc.

Illustrations by Michael Gellatly

Book design by Christina Gaugler

Library of Congress Cataloging-in-Publication Data

Remy, Mark.
    The runner's field manual : a tactical (and practical) survival guide/ by Mark Remy and the Editors of Runner's World.
        p.   cm.
    Includes index.
    ISBN-13 978–1–60529–272–4 hardcover
    1. Running—Handbooks, manuals, etc.   I. Runner's world (Emmaus, Pa. : 1987)
II. Title.
    GV1061.R44 2010
    796.42—dc22   2010020241

Distributed to the trade by Macmillan

2 4 6 8 10 9 7 5 3 1 hardcover

We inspire and enable people to improve their lives and the world around them.
www.rodalebooks.com

For Beatrice

This *Field Manual* belongs to:

_____

Contents

Acknowledgments

After writing my first book, *The Runner's Rule Book,* I joked that the experience was like running a marathon: There was the looming, daunting goal; the weeks and months of plodding work; and finally an agonizing sprint to the finish. At which point I was exhausted . . . and ready to do it again.

And so I did.

Writing *The Runner's Field Manual* proved to be another marathon, for sure. Many people helped me reach this particular finish line. I'd like to thank some of them here.

Thanks to the fans and spectators—everyone who read the *Rule Book* and told me that they enjoyed it, as well as the readers of my *RunnersWorld.com* blog, RW Daily. Your encouragement was, and is, a tremendous help.

Thanks to the organizers—*Runner's World* Editor-in-Chief David Willey, who did so much to help make the *Field Manual* a reality; John Atwood, my editor for the book, whose suggestions (big and small) brought each chapter into sharper focus; Christina Gaugler, whose design direction breathed life into each page; and the entire Rodale Books team.

Thanks to my training partners, the staff here at *Runner's World*—working with you has made me a better writer and editor than I could ever be on my own.

Last but not least: Thanks to my wife, Sarah, who indulged my many Saturdays holed up at the library and endured my occasional anxiety and crabbiness with patience and grace.

I'm spent. Let's do it again!

The Runner's Oath

On my honor I will do my best

To be a better runner;

To watch for cars, and increase my mileage gradually;

To run in the rain, without boast or complaint;

To not go out way too fast;

To eat right, listen to my body, and,

one of these days, volunteer at a race.

Introduction

Hello! Welcome to *The Runner's Field Manual.*

Look carefully at the group of people to the left. Can you spot the runner? If you answered, "None of these people are runners," you are correct. The runner is out doing a long run because she has a half-marathon next month and doesn't have time to just stand around posing with a group of strangers.

The point is that running requires dedication, if you want to do it right. It also requires a certain base of practical, real-world knowledge—of "how-to" information that will keep you happy and healthy.

For instance . . .

How do you know what shoes to buy? (See page 48.) How long should you sit in an ice bath? (Not one moment longer than you have to; page 143.) Is there a right way and a wrong way to run downhill? (Oh, yes; page 31.) How do you know if you're dressed properly for the conditions? (Check page 59.)

And for the love of Bowerman, how can you keep your shoelaces from coming untied, once and for all? (Page 55.)

My goal with *The Runner's Field Manual* is to address all of these questions and many more—including, I hope, a few questions you never knew you had. And to make you smile a few times along the way.

Put another way: Whereas my previous book, *The Runner's Rule Book*, told you things, *The Runner's Field Manual* will *show* you. At least that's my aim.

The information and advice that follows is intended not just for newbies, but for anyone who wants to learn a little more about the craft of running and the art of being a runner. Think of it as the set of instructions you wish you'd gotten with your very first pair of running shoes.

Enjoy.

—Mark Remy

Chapter 1

The Basics

Anybody can run. To see this principle in action, head to your local mall, purchase a dozen brown mice at the pet store, then release them in the food court. See? Running is easy.

Becoming a runner, on the other hand . . . well, that's not so simple. Becoming a runner takes discipline, a little know-how, and a lot of patience.

The Runner's Field Manual can't help you with the discipline or patience. But we can help you with the know-how. We'll start in this chapter by addressing a few of the fundamentals, beginning with some basic questions.

Who Is a "Runner"?

A runner, broadly speaking, is anyone who runs. Simple as that. Don't let anyone tell you anything different.

What Is Running?

This is a basic question, with a basic answer.

Running is defined as moving at any pace faster than a walk. More technically: If both feet are off the ground at any given moment while you're moving, then you are running. Conversely, if you have at least one foot on the ground at all times, then by definition, you are walking.

It should be noted that this seemingly straightforward issue has become fraught with tension and even, occasionally, anger. Some "back-of-the-packers," particularly those who employ a run/walk strategy while training or racing, sense a value judgment here and bristle at the suggestion that they aren't "real" runners. That's unfortunate, and such anger is misguided, for several reasons.

First, there is no shame in walking, and to imply otherwise is itself insulting to anyone who walks for fun and fitness. Second, this is a question of mechanics . . . not of speed or dedication or anything else.

(Elite racewalkers can walk—yes, walk—at a 6-minute-per-mile pace.) Certainly it's not a question of anyone's character. Third, and finally, isn't it a little silly to fret over semantics and labels? Why not use that energy instead to just get out there and get moving?

Someday Merriam-Webster may change its definitions of running and walking. Until it does, *The Runner's Field Manual* will stick with the ones we have, and move on—at whatever pace we can manage.

Where Should You Run?

You should run wherever you're able to run, and wherever you enjoy running—assuming it's legal and reasonably safe, for you and those around you.

Most runners use *public streets and roads*. Since this chapter is titled "The Basics," we'll go ahead and say it: Running on highways and freeways usually isn't legal and never is safe. If you find yourself stopped at a toll plaza during a run, you have definitely strayed into inappropriate territory.

Many runners enjoy running on *trails*, away from traffic and the "hustle and bustle" of modern life. The word *trail* can mean an

---

F.Y.I.

Go Against the Flow

Here's another bit of basic knowledge: Pedestrians, including runners, should walk or run *against* traffic—not with it. Not only is this the law in most places, it's just good common sense: It's much easier to see and respond to traffic when you're facing it than when it's constantly zooming up behind you.

unpaved path in a public park, a highly technical singletrack on a mountainside, or anything in between. We'll discuss trail running in more detail in Chapter 2.

Typically paved routes through parks or along bodies of water, *paths* are a nice option. Just be aware that most such paths are designed for "mixed use"—so keep an eye out for walkers, in-line skaters, and cyclists, as well as other runners. [Fig. A]

For city dwellers, running on *sidewalks* is inevitable (e.g., you might need to run on the sidewalk to get to a nearby park or gym) but is best kept to a minimum. Very few people enjoy running on sidewalks, for a variety of reasons. They can be crowded with walkers, baby strollers, and so on; they're often narrow; they may be cracked

Fig. A

or uneven or littered with debris, all of which can trip you; and so on. If you must run on a sidewalk, watch your step.

The *outdoor track* is perfectly suited for speed workouts, or for any run where precision and consistency count—it's easy on a track to check your pace and time your "splits" every 200, 400, or 800 meters. And hey, there are no hills or traffic. Just be sure you have permission to use the track, and be courteous to any other runners or walkers sharing it with you. *Note:* If you find yourself constantly dodging stock cars or greyhounds, you are on the wrong sort of track; find another.

Of course, you can run indoors as well, either on a *treadmill* or an *indoor track*. Both present challenges—treadmills can be dull, and there may be a wait to use them; indoor tracks may be crowded, and are often short and steeply banked, which can result in injuries if you're not careful. Or even if you are.

When Should You Run?

From a practical and personal point of view, you should run whenever you're able to make the time for it and whenever you're most likely to actually do it. (For example: Don't plan an after-work run when you know you have a late meeting that's liable to go long; instead, set the alarm extra early and get it done before work.)

From a statistical risk point of view, there are a few times you ought to avoid running, if possible. Late at night, for instance, or in the very early morning after a holiday—times that drunken drivers are more likely to be on the roads. Also notoriously risky: the first morning of daylight saving time, when drivers are groggy from "springing ahead" one hour the night before. We'll explore other hazards, and how to protect yourself from them, in Chapters 2 and 6.

Marathon Mania

You'll notice that Chapter 1 of this book is titled "The Basics." It is not titled "Marathoning." This is deliberate.

For better or for worse, the marathon has exploded in popularity in recent years. New marathons are popping up left and right, and existing races are filling up in record time, despite rising prices. One factor driving this is the growing number of first-time marathoners.

The Runner's Field Manual is happy to see so many people taking an interest in running. After all, if there's one thing Americans could use more of, it's exercise. But the nearly fetishistic frenzy now surrounding the marathon distance is troubling. In fact, it could backfire in a big way. When inexperienced runners rush headlong into a 26.2-mile foot race, they epitomize "doing too much, too soon." (See Number One Rule, opposite page.) Their risk of injury or burnout is quite high.

This is sad. Ironic, too, because one lesson the marathon can teach us is the importance of patience, of taking the long view. *The Runner's Field Manual* wishes more beginning runners would take this lesson to heart before they dive into their first marathon. Be patient. Race shorter distances for a year, two years, or more. Build a strong foundation. And *then* consider a marathon. (Or not. *The Runner's Field Manual* has it on good authority that many runners lead long, healthy, happy lives without ever having raced 26.2 miles. Strange, but true!)

The message for newbies, in short: The marathon has been around for a long time. It will be here for a long time to come. So what's your rush?

Why Should You Run?

Why should you run? Come on. You might as well ask, "Why breathe?"

Why Breathe?

The Runner's Field Manual will not dignify that with a response.

How Do You Get Started?

You start running the way you start anything: from the beginning. Picking up *The Runner's Field Manual* is a good start. Congratulations! But there are many valuable resources out there for the beginning runner, or for anyone who just wants to learn more about running. *Runner's World* publishes an excellent magazine and Web site (*RunnersWorld.com*), as well as books on everything from training to nutrition. Joining a local running club is a tremendous way to learn the ropes, too—and to make some new friends.

What's the Number One Rule Any New Runner Should Remember?

The Runner's Field Manual is glad you asked. The number one rule that any new runner should remember, far and away, is this: Don't do too much, too soon.

That's it. Simple. *Don't do too much, too soon.* No new runner ever got hurt by starting a running program too slowly, or by progressing too gradually.

Because so many beginners—in their eagerness and enthusiasm—forget or ignore this rule, and because the consequences of forgetting or ignoring it often lead to injury or burnout or both, we'll repeat it once more: Don't do too much, too soon.

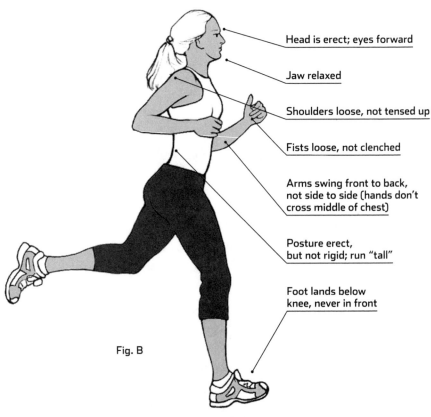

Head is erect; eyes forward

Jaw relaxed

Shoulders loose, not tensed up

Fists loose, not clenched

Arms swing front to back,
not side to side (hands don't
cross middle of chest)

Posture erect,
but not rigid; run "tall"

Foot lands below
knee, never in front

Fig. B

Running Form

The proper way to run is whatever way moves you along with the most ease, comfort, and speed. Usually this happens to be the way that comes to you naturally.

This is true despite the reams of research and opinion (mostly opinion) on the superiority of such-and-such style of running, or the evils of such-and-such other style of running. And despite what adherents to any one style of running may preach.

This is not to say that your form can't evolve, or that you shouldn't experiment with various sorts of running, or that you shouldn't try tweaking your stride or your footstrike or your arm swing or whatever. You should. Just introduce these tweaks slowly and subtly, and pay attention to your body's feedback.

This is also not to say that a handful of broad principles don't apply to most any "proper" running form. They do. [See Fig. B.] But just a handful. And very broad.

For instance, generally speaking, you want as much of your energy as possible to translate into forward motion. This means minimizing lateral (side-to-side) movement, and trying not to bounce too much with each step. Energy spent swinging your arms left to right, or springing into the air with each step, is energy not spent moving you down the road.

In the end, only you can decide what your running form should look and feel like. Remember that and you'll be fine.

Some Commonly Seen Gaits

Running form varies greatly from person to person. It can also be a very individual thing, to the point where you may be able to identify certain of your running friends in the distance, just by the way they're running.

Still, the longer you run, the more you'll notice a handful of basic running styles cropping up again and again. Here are a few.

The Scuff-n-Shuffle. Maybe his shoes are heavy. Maybe he figures the lower he keeps his feet to the ground, the more energy he'll preserve for forward motion. Maybe he's just exhausted. Whatever the reason, this runner scuffs along with his soles scraping the road, never achieving more than a few millimeters' worth of elevation. The upshot: This guy will never startle you when he passes. You'll hear him a mile away.

Fig. C

The Dance of the Dangling Arms (a.k.a. the Invisible-Suitcase Carrier). Arm swing? Not for her, thanks. [Fig. C]

The Super Stooper. Usually, but not always, this runner is elderly, God bless him. Probably dressed in cotton sweats or even in street clothes, he plods along bent forward at the waist. You silently worry that he'll run into a tree or something, since he appears to be staring at the ground. But hey, if he's survived this long, he must know what he's doing.

The Freakishly Severe Inward Foot Roll. This person may be moving along okay, with no apparent discomfort. But man, just watching her feet slap and roll inward on the pavement is enough to make *you* cringe. Ouch.

The Air Puncher. He may be moving fast or slow, his face calm or (more often) etched in pain. The one constant: His arms are all over the place. In the most common variation, he seems to be delivering a series of left and right hook punches as he moves forward. Hitting the air out of his way, maybe? Your guess is as good as ours, because we're afraid to get near enough to ask.

The Bounder. When you see this classic overstrider, you'll wonder whether he imagines we get only a finite number of strides in our lifetime, so we may as well make the most of each one. More likely he just doesn't know that whenever the foot lands in front of the knee, it acts as a brake—slowing you down and making your run a lot harder (and more jarring) than it has to be.

Training Plans

Here's a basic fact of running: Entering a race (of any distance) is a beautiful way to motivate yourself to run. And having a training plan is the best way to train for a race.

A training plan from a trusted source—such as, oh, RunnersWorld.com's SmartCoach tool or Training Plan Store—is good because it takes the guesswork out. You find your plan, work backward from the date of your race, then . . . follow the plan. Nothing could be simpler.

That said, don't feel you have to follow your plan to the letter, every single mile of every single day, no matter what. *The Runner's Field Manual* advises against this overly rigid approach—for the sake of your own sanity. You don't want to wind up like those people who not only can't cook anything without a recipe, but can't cook anything without following that recipe to the point of counting individual pecans or adding flour with atomically calibrated measuring cups. What fun is that?

So, relax. If you run 5.2 (or 4.6) miles one day instead of 5 miles, it's okay. If you must miss a run altogether, because of illness or injury or any reason whatsoever, don't sweat it. Resume training when you can, and move on.

Quick Tip

As noted in Rule 1.26 of our previous book, *The Runner's Rule Book* (Rodale, 2009), training plans should be printed out and displayed on your refrigerator. Not only does this provide a daily, eye-level reminder of your goals, it also might help to deter you from reaching into the fridge for that hunk of chocolate chip cheesecake. (Note: We said *might*.)

Common Threats

The world being what it is, the modern runner faces several threats in the field, ranging from annoying to downright dangerous. We will address each of these in more detail later in the book, but here is a sneak peak at a few of the most common.

- Cracked sidewalks (See Chapter 2: Urban, Suburban & Wilderness Survival)
- Underdressing/hypothermia (Chapter 3: Shoes, Gear & Apparel)
- Pints of premium ice cream (Chapter 4: Foraging & Sustenance)
- Oblivious fellow runners (Chapter 5: Running with Others)
- Motorists (Chapter 6: Dealing with Motorists)
- Blisters and chafing (Chapter 7: Health, Safety & First Aid)
- Finish-line vomit (Chapter 8: Racing)

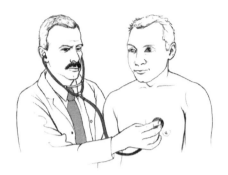

First, See Your Doctor

"Before you start any exercise program, consult your physician."

You read or hear this advice all the time. Maybe so often that you tend to ignore it. You shouldn't.

Seeing a doctor before you begin any sort of strenuous exercise program is a simple, painless, commonsense step. Don't assume, for instance, that because you "ran in school," you can jump back into running today, months or years later.

And certainly anytime you sign up for a big race—half-marathon distance or longer, for sure—your physician should know what you're up to. Have your doc check you out, and share the following information with him or her:

◆ Your own athletic background and health history

◆ Any preexisting conditions; family record of health problems; and current medical concerns or questions (including things like allergies, asthma, etc.)

◆ All medications you're currently taking or have recently taken, and why, including over-the-counter meds

◆ What event(s) you're training for—when, where, and what distance

◆ What sort of training plan you intend to follow

Once the doc gives you the green light, you're ready to run!

How to Run

We've saved the single most basic lesson of this chapter for last: how to run. This is a two-step lesson.

Step 1: Start running.

Step 2: Keep running.

Congratulations! You've got it!

Now let's move on to some more advanced topics.

EARN THE BADGE: **Running 101**

Requirements

1. Explain the difference between running and walking, without actually doing either.

2. Name four places you might run, and cite the pros and cons of each.

3. Create a side-view drawing of a runner showing proper running form. Use arrows to point out where and how proper form is being followed.

4. Write a script for a cautionary public service announcement titled "Too Much, Too Soon."

5. Talk to a doctor about your running. Be sure to discuss how much you run, how often, how intensely, etc., and to mention any history of health problems. If you can't find a doctor, talk to somebody who resembles one.

6. Locate a brand-new runner who is thinking about signing up for a marathon. Persuade him not to, without using the words *should, shouldn't,* or *insane.*

Notes

Chapter 2

Urban, Suburban & Wilderness Survival

Relatively speaking, running is an extremely safe activity. Compared with rock climbing, mountain biking, or football, heading out for a run is practically risk free. Still, threats do exist. And there is plenty you can (and should) do to avoid them. In this chapter, we'll explore ways to remain happy, healthy, and intact wherever you happen to be running.

In this chapter, we'll examine the good, the bad, and the ugly of running in each of three main environments: city; suburban; and rural/wilderness. We'll also offer specific advice for running at night, on the beach, and indoors, as well as tips for running in all four seasons.

Finally, we'll consider the single most important survival skill of all, no matter who you are or where you're running: the ability to relieve yourself anywhere, with minimal risk of danger and embarrassment.

Let's start by listing a few common items that no runner should be without.

The Runner's Survival Kit

Just like a Boy Scout, a good runner is always prepared. With that in mind, here are a few things you should keep handy.

AT HOME

- Adhesive bandages
- Needles, straight pins, safety pins (for popping blisters)
- Rubbing alcohol (for sterilizing those popping implements)
- Antibacterial cream
- Petroleum jelly

- Antacid tablets
- Sunscreen
- Toenail clippers
- Nail scissors
- Nail file
- Tea tree oil (dab some in between your toes, or inside old shoes, to keep funky smells at bay)

- Lavender oil (a few drops on your bed linens may help you fall asleep)
- Duct tape (some runners use it to tape nipples to protect them from friction, or to cover blisters)

IN YOUR CAR TRUNK

- An old pair of running shoes (for those impromptu running opportunities, or in case something horrible happens to your shoes before, say, the start of a local race)

- Washcloths or small towel, plus baby wipes (for postrun or postrace cleanup)

- Set of old clothes, e.g., shorts, pants, T-shirt (for changing into something dry postrun or postrace)

- Toilet paper (better safe than sorry)

- Old space blankets from races

IN YOUR RACE-WEEKEND SUITCASE

- Safety pins
- Petroleum jelly or body lube
- Adhesive bandages or nipple guards
- Antacid tablets
- Sunscreen
- Spare contact lenses, if you wear them

- Race confirmation card
- Extra pair of running shoes, just in case
- Plenty of whatever gels, chews, bars, or sports drinks you favor
- Large trash bags, to wear in case of rain on race morning (see page 61)

- Old tube socks, which can be cut into improvised disposable arm warmers (see page 60)
- Earplugs (in case you find yourself stuck with loud neighbors at the hotel)

ON YOUR PERSON, DURING A RUN

- Identification (wristband, shoelace tag, etc.), including name, blood type, any allergies, and emergency contact

- $10 for emergencies

- Cell phone, if you don't mind carrying one

IN YOUR HEAD

- A good supply of common sense and a healthy dose of wariness. Plus, of course, the knowledge contained in this book.

Quick Tip

Home remedy alert! *The Runner's Field Manual* hasn't tried it firsthand, but some runners swear that Preparation H works well to dry up blisters.

Common Threats

For the runner, survival tactics are largely dependent on the environment you're running in. The urban runner faces different threats than the suburban runner, and the wilderness/trail runner's challenges are different still. Here's a list of some of the things you'll need to watch out for, broken down by setting.

Urban

◆ The dive-bombing, law-ignoring bicycle messenger [Fig. A]

◆ The big shot businessman staring at his BlackBerry as he walks

◆ Bus and truck exhaust

◆ The panhandler

◆ Tourists who walk three or more abreast and stop without warning

◆ Dog poo

◆ Sidewalk cracks [Fig. B]

Fig. A

◆ Potholes large enough to swallow a taxicab

◆ The taxicab

◆ The street performer

◆ The pedicab, which combines the hazards of the bicycle messenger and the taxicab

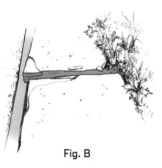

Fig. B

EARN THE BADGE: URBAN RUNNING

Requirements

① During a run, find a business with a sign reading "Rest room for customers only" and persuade the staff to let you use it.

② Volunteer at a local race.

③ Learn to scream "Watch where you're driving!" in at least five foreign languages.

④ Using geometry and basic math, calculate how many feet you add to your average run in your efforts to avoid groups of smokers on the sidewalk.

⑤ Map the shortest possible route from your apartment to the park, taking into account lights, bus routes, traffic patterns, etc. Be prepared to defend your route.

⑥ Memorize the locations of all specialty running stores in your city, with cross streets.

Suburban

- The parent driving her over-scheduled child in an SUV while talking on a cell phone

- The motorist backing out of his driveway at 28 mph

- The bored, angry dog [Fig. C]

- Dog poo

- Tricycles and scooters

Fig. C

- Balls of various types and sizes

- Strollers

- Sprinklers

- Those clouds of tiny gnats (or whatever they are) that you sometimes encounter

- Thieves who loiter in parking lots near parks or trails popular with runners

- Lawn care workers who would just as soon maul you with their 72-inch-deck mowers as wait for you to pass on the sidewalk

- Apoplectic motorists who are angry that the streets are closed temporarily for a race, even though they're probably just driving a mile to the supermarket and the road closures were announced repeatedly in local media for days leading up to the event

Wilderness/Trail

- Snakes, bears, wolves, and so forth (a.k.a. "wildlife")

- Holes

- Rocks

- Roots [Fig. D]

- Fallen (or falling) branches

- The hunter ½ mile away whose rifle has a range of 1 mile

Fig. D

- The mountain biker who has watched too many Mountain Dew commercials

- The escaped mental patient with hooks instead of hands who killed a runner out here, years back, on a day just like this one

Caution!

Retractable Dog Leashes

Dogs are usually less of a threat when they're on a leash. Not so when their owners opt for adjustable, retractable leashes over the old-fashioned, static kind.

A retractable leash consists of a large plastic handle, from which a narrow cord unspools, attaching to a dog's collar. These cords, some of which can reach 25 feet when fully extended, are sometimes so narrow as to be nearly invisible, forming a sort of doggy tripwire for unwitting walkers or runners.

Next time you approach a human and a dog during a run, look closely before passing between them. Better yet, go around them if you can. The doggy tripwire takes no prisoners.

How Not to Die Alone in the Woods If, God Forbid, Your Fancy GPS Watch Goes Kaput

Global positioning systems are wonderful. But they can become crutches, allowing your "old school" navigation skills to atrophy. They can also foster a false sense of security, encouraging some walkers, backpackers, and runners to venture into remote places they probably shouldn't—particularly if the weather is poor or threatens to become so, and especially if they're venturing out solo. This is foolish, because even the most advanced GPS system can fail or become inoperable.

If you found yourself alone in the woods with a useless GPS, would you know how to get your bearings? Here's a refresher course.

+ **The sun rises in the east and sets in the west.** (Don't laugh; sometimes the most basic knowledge is the first to go.) At noon, the sun will be in the south (in the Northern Hemisphere) or in the north (in the Southern Hemisphere).

♦ **If the moon rises before sunset, the lighted side will face west.** If it rises after midnight, the lighted side will be facing east.

♦ **Power lines and railroad tracks lead to civilization.** Or something close to it.

♦ **People who are lost really do tend to walk in circles.** Keep this in mind if you're trying to maintain a straight course home. Use a series of landmarks in the distance to stay straight.

♦ **Don't rely on moss.** The old adage that moss always grows on the north side of trees isn't really accurate.

Finally, remember that heading into the wilderness by yourself is never a smart thing to do—but if you do head out alone, be sure to tell a friend or loved one exactly where you're going and when to expect you back.

The Year-Round Runner

Whether you live in a climate that's scorching, freezing, parched, or drenched, there's no reason you can't run safely and enjoyably year-round. You just need to make a few commonsense adjustments. The following suggestions are a good place to start.

Running in the Cold

Your two main tasks when running in cold weather are to stay warm and dry, and to remain upright. Staying warm and dry mostly means dressing right (see "Dressing for Any Condition," page 59). Cotton is a no-no in cold weather—especially next to the skin—because it retains moisture, and moisture plus cold equals bad news. Instead,

Build a Runner Snowman

When you're done running in the snow, here's another way to have fun in it.

1. Construct a standard snowman, with large base, medium-size middle, and smaller head; energy chew eyes; energy bar mouth; etc.

2. Add sticks for arms; strap old running watch on one "wrist."

3. In front, scoop out two holes at the bottom of the base; insert old running shoes.

4. Attach bib number on midsection.

5. Cap or visor is optional.

6. For added effect, stand a card table next to your snow runner and cover it with cups of water.

wear synthetic, wicking layers and a breathable jacket that will let sweat escape while keeping precipitation out.

Other tips:

- Wear easily visible clothing, since drivers won't be expecting many runners to be out in such unpleasant conditions. Bright reds and oranges contrast nicely with snow.

- A layer of petroleum jelly will help to protect exposed skin, such as the face.

- Take short steps, with knees very slightly bent, to increase your stability on slick roads and sidewalks.

- If ice is widespread, use removable cleats, such as Yaktrax, to increase your grip. If you're in a DIY mood, you can also try sinking small screws into the bottoms of your shoes.

- Begin your run into the wind whenever possible, so that you aren't facing a cold headwind on the way back, when you're likely to be sweaty.

- Change into dry clothing ASAP upon finishing your run.

The Zipper as Thermostat

When you're running in weather that's cold bordering on cool, especially if it's also windy, reach for clothing with zippers. Tops, jackets, and vests with zippers are your best friends in inclement weather. You'll be amazed at how much you can adjust your body temperature on the run, simply by finessing a zipper—or zippers—up and down as needed, depending on changes in ambient temperature, direction of the wind, uphill versus downhill running, and so on. In cold weather, *The Runner's Field Manual* prefers a midzip, long-sleeve, wicking top paired with a full-length-zip shell.

Running in the Heat

A hot, humid run can really sap your energy, if you aren't prepared for it. So prepare. Fluids are key, of course. Stay hydrated throughout the day. (But not overhydrated—see "Caution! Water Overload," page 28.) Run by feel, slowing your pace as needed to cope with the warmth. And keep cool with these tips as well:

◆ Acclimate to the heat as gradually as you can. If you're racing in a warm climate but were unable to train in those conditions, at least try to arrive a few days early and get in one or two runs. And adjust your race goals accordingly.

◆ Try to do most of your running in the early morning or the evening, when temperatures are lower.

◆ Plan your routes to pass water fountains or locations where you can pause to buy water or a sports drink. For a long run in a rural area, drive the course the night before and stash bottles along the way.

◆ If you begin to feel nauseated, light-headed, or dizzy, or if you stop sweating, *end your run immediately.* Seek shade and a cool drink, and see a doctor if symptoms don't improve.

F.Y.I.

The National Weather Service considers it dangerous to exercise when the heat and humidity meet (or exceed) these combinations:

HEAT / HUMIDITY

86°F / 90%

88°F / 80%

90°F / 70%

92°F / 60%

94°F / 55%

96°F / 45%

98°F / 40%

Running in the Rain

Running in the rain—whether a gentle misting or a downpour—can actually be fun. After all, once you're soaked, it's not as if you'll get any wetter. And the fair-weather runners will be indoors, waiting for fair weather. Which leaves more room on the roads and trails for you. Just remember a few simple tips to stay safe.

- Dress for it. This means a billed baseball cap to keep rain out of your eyes, and a light, breathable jacket or vest, even if it's relatively warm. (When you're wet, hypothermia is a much greater risk.) Just as with cold-weather running, the more visible you are, the better; brightly colored rain jackets are best.

- Watch out for stuff underfoot that turns slippery when wet. This means painted lines, metal grates, leaves, maybe even the road surface itself. It can be surprisingly easy to wipe out on rain-slick surfaces.

Caution! Water Overload

It is possible to overhydrate. Drinking too much water may lead to a potentially life-threatening condition called hyponatremia, wherein the body's sodium levels become dangerously low and cells (including those in the brain) swell.

Hyponatremia has become more common among runners in recent years, as larger numbers of slower runners enter marathons. They are often on the course for many hours at a time, drinking as much as possible for fear of becoming dehydrated.

The old rule to "drink before you're thirsty" is just that: an old rule. Instead, drink *when* you're thirsty. Don't overdo it. And whenever possible, opt for a sports drink, which contains sodium, over plain water.

- Take it easy down hills. You may want to shorten your stride a bit, too—again, because the road will be slicker than usual.

- Don't forget to hydrate. Sometimes drinking is the last thing on your mind when you're wet all over. Remind yourself that external fluids don't cancel out the need for the internal variety.

- As with cold-weather running, change into dry clothing ASAP upon finishing your run.

Running in a Hurricane

We have just one tip for running in a hurricane: Don't.

Perhaps you could burn some calories nailing plywood over your windows instead?

Running in Perfect Weather

Sun, low humidity, gentle breeze, and temperatures in the low 60s? Hey, the biggest risk here is not pausing occasionally to appreciate it.

Fig. E

Checking Yourself Out

Large picture windows and glass storefronts allow a passing runner a rare chance to glance over and check himself out while he's running. [Fig. E] (A row of parked cars offers the same thing, but only from the chest up.) If a fellow runner sees you doing this and taunts you, just say that you're only "checking your form," and quickly change the subject.

Just watch where you're going—nothing ruins your form faster than running full speed into a lamppost or mailbox.

Running Uphill, Running Downhill

Any time you run uphill or downhill, you will need to adjust the basic running form we outlined in Chapter 1 (page 8). But just slightly. Many of the same principles apply: Stay loose and relaxed, maintain a front-to-back arm swing (not side-to-side), run "tall."

Beyond those universals, here are a few things to keep in mind when you are . . .

Running Uphill

◆ Shorten your stride and run more on your forefeet than usual.

◆ Spring up and off the hill—not into it; think "light and springy."

◆ Run within yourself for the first two-thirds of the hill; save some energy to push through the final bit.

◆ Try a mantra, such as "up and over, up and over."

Q&A

Q: If a hill plateaus for a bit before rising again, is it considered a single long hill? Or multiple shorter ones?

A: Now, that is a tricky question. To *The Runner's Field Manual*'s, knowledge, there is no official, scientific way to answer that. So here is our own unofficial, unscientific answer: If the plateau in question is long enough for a runner's breathing and heart rate to return to a relatively normal range before climbing resumes, you're dealing with two (or more) hills. If not, you're climbing a single, long hill that happens to include a short break.

- Most important: Work *with* the hill, not against it. Tensing up and "attacking" a climb is a waste of energy. The hill will win every time.

Running Downhill

- Take short, quick steps, with your feet landing beneath you. Over-striding while running downhill is dangerous and inefficient.

- Keep your arm swing shorter than usual. This will help you keep your stride short.

- Decompress; take advantage of this "down" time to breathe deeply and shake out your arms.

- Scan the road for debris, rocks, ruts, etc., a bit farther ahead than usual, to account for your increased speed.

The 5 Types of Hills

The Long Grind. It's not that steep, for the most part. But man, it just goes on. And on. And on . . .

The Short and Sweet. Even if it's steep (which it might not be), this one is over before you know it.

The False Summit. Whew! That was a rough climb. At least it's almost over. Oh, wait . . . no it's not. Cripes.

The Switchbacker. The cool way it zigzags upward almost makes up for the pain it inflicts.

The Wall. If you catch yourself wondering whether walking this one might be faster than running it, you're dealing with a Wall.

Q&A

Q: Should I weight train? Will lifting weights make me a better runner?

A: Well, that's actually two questions. But we'll allow it. Few experts would argue against resistance training. Pretty much anyone can benefit from it, providing it's done safely and properly, and not *overdone*. Will it make you a better runner? That depends on what kind of weight training you do, and how much. And even on your definition of "better runner."

A few general rules for distance runners: For beginners, machines are generally safer than free weights; a good, steep hill run will build leg strength better than any machine will; and it's hard to improve on the classic pushup.

Navigating the Gym

No matter where you live or where you do most of your running, chances are good you'll find yourself at a gym sooner or later. That said, you likely won't spend a lot of time there, relative to the time you'll spend outdoors. So *The Runner's Field Manual* won't spend much time there, either.

Here is all you need to know.

- The man who has been on the treadmill for 48 minutes, flipping idly through *People* magazine as he strolls at 1.5 mph, will not get off just because you glare at him.

- But you might as well glare anyway.

- If you're tempted to turn your music up loud enough to drown out the music emanating from another gym-goer's earbuds, you're usually better off giving up and listening to the other guy's music.

- Elliptical trainers deliver none of the impact that treadmills do, while preserving 100 percent of the boredom.

- If you have a knack for always choosing the wobbly shopping cart at the supermarket, this skill will transfer to the gym, where you will wind up on the one treadmill that shakes so hard you can hear it in the parking lot.

Fig. F

Q&A

Q: What's the deal with that little red clip-on thingy that attaches to the treadmill console with a little cord?

A: That is an emergency power cutoff thingy. Or, in more technical terms, an emergency power cutoff thingamajig. The idea is to clip one end somewhere on your person so that if you slip or trip, the cord will yank free from the console, cutting the treadmill's power and saving you from certain doom.

It won't save you from mortifying embarrassment, though. So *The Runner's Field Manual* recommends not slipping or tripping in the first place.

- You may think, while you're doing it, that treadmill running is harder than running outdoors. It isn't.

- If you think that flip-flops will save you from the nasty stuff floating around in the showers, you are deluding yourself.

Treadmill Survival

The treadmill [Fig. F] can be a valuable training tool. For those runners who can't train outdoors, it's a lifesaver. But the treadmill can also injure you (if you're not careful) or sap your will to live (even if you are careful).

Treadmill risk can be divided into two main categories: physical and mental.

- **Physical risks** include stumbling, falling, or otherwise doing something klutzy, up to and including a full-on George Jetson–style slip off the back of the speeding belt. In real life, this is never as comical as it sounds. In fact, it can result in serious injury. So watch your step.

- The treadmill's **mental risks** are less apparent but just as dangerous. The main risk here is sheer boredom, which can reach toxic levels in as little as 10 minutes for those unprepared for, or unaccustomed to, the treadmill. Legend has it that one of the original treadmill testers, in the early 20th century, grew so despondent that, weeping, he stopped and tried to beat himself unconscious with his own shoe. (Remember, this was nearly a century before cell phones made it possible to run next to a stranger having a loud, 20-minute conversation about her bowel obstruction, and whether she should cut her hair "super short" or keep it shoulder length.)

Primarily due to these mental hazards, *The Runner's Field Manual* prefers, as a personal matter, to avoid treadmills whenever possible. Should you insist on using one, the best ways to stay sane are to watch television while you run; listen to music, podcasts, or an audiobook; and/or vary the pace and incline relatively often, to relieve the monotony.

Running at Night

To the uninitiated, nighttime running might sound like a needless danger. Anyone who's tried it, however, knows how much fun it can be, and how exhilarating. And it's just as safe as daytime running, if you follow a few simple precautions.

Most obviously, make yourself as visible as possible. This means wearing reflective clothing or a reflective vest, and using at least one light. (Headlamps are a popular option, as they leave your hands free and aim a shaft of light wherever you happen to be facing.)

The Visibility Index

When you're running in the dark, at what distance will a driver first see you? It depends on how you're outfitted. Here's how far away you'll be spotted, based on what you're wearing, from a *Runner's World* field test.

½ **MILE:** Drivers can detect a headlamp or a handheld light. The whitish beam combined with its motion helps drivers recognize you as a runner.

¼ **MILE:** At this distance, drivers will see a reflective vest or a blinking red light. The light should have a bright LED.

150 YARDS: A brightly colored jacket or top will attract a driver's attention. Yellowish green or bright orange is best. Reflective panels on sleeves help, too.

50 FEET: Although a white T-shirt becomes visible before a dark one does, the difference is negligible—especially if a driver is speeding.

30–40 FEET: Wearing dark pants and a dark shirt? You are practically invisible to drivers, who likely won't notice you until it's too late.

Just as important: Assume that, to drivers, you are invisible. Be hypervigilant. And leave the MP3 player at home.

Encountering Wild Animals

You're running—in the woods or in a race or wherever—when you spot a large bear. Quick! What do you do? Well, the first step is to determine whether it really is a bear. Are you sure it's not just a fellow runner *dressed* as a bear? Use these field tests to find out.

- **Look at his feet.** Real bears rarely wear shoes; runners dressed as bears often do.

- **Examine his stools.** A real bear's fecal matter will contain things like berries, fish, and possibly garbage left by campers, and can be found lying in mounds in the woods. The feces of a runner in a costume, whose stool will be harder to locate, will have traces of energy gels, pasta, and Pop-Tarts.

- **Just ask.** Approach the creature and say, "Are you a real bear? Or a runner in a costume?" If he replies, "I'm a person," you're good. (Come to think of it, if he replies, "I'm a bear," you're probably also good.) If he mauls you, it's a real bear.

A Word about Roadkill

Sooner or later, as a runner, you will come upon a dead animal in the road. [Fig. G]

Unless you recognize the animal in question ("Mr. Whiskers?") your only obligation here is to circumvent the thing safely and without retching. Here's how.

As you approach the carcass, begin taking deep breaths about 15 feet away. When you're approximately 6 feet away, exhale, take a final, deep breath, then hold it. (Imagine yourself jumping feet first into the deep end of a swimming pool—but instead of water, you'll be submerged in stink.)

Stay relaxed and maintain your normal pace. After a few strides, release the air slowly from pursed lips. But don't breathe in just yet. A few strides more, and you should be safely out of range. You may resume your normal breathing pattern.

Fig. G

Running on Vacation

Should you run while away on vacation? Here is a rule of thumb: If you're asking yourself, "*Should* I run while on vacation?" the answer is almost always no.

That's because the word *should* connotes a certain sense of dread or—at the very least—a serious lack of oomph. And you know what's great at getting that oomph back? A break from running! Of course, some vacationers plan their trips around running—for instance, signing up for a destination marathon, then taking a few extra days before and after the race to relax. Which is perfectly fine, too, if that idea excites you. Bon voyage.

Running on the Beach

It's not for everyone, and it's rarely as idyllic as you imagine it. But if it's done right, running on the beach can be fun and rewarding. Here are some pointers.

+ **Run at low tide.** The receding water will have left a reasonably smooth, hard-packed surface. Running at high tide will mean dealing with deep, dry, shifting sand higher up on the beach.

+ **Go out and back.** Most beaches are on at least a slight slant. Because running on an angled surface can be tough on knees and hips, run out halfway, then turn around to return. That way you'll share the stress evenly between your left and right sides.

Q&A

Dealing with Dead Bodies

If newspaper accounts are to be believed, runners and joggers discover approximately 60 percent of dead bodies found outdoors. [Fig. H] If you find one, how should you react? Here are answers to some common questions.

Q: How will I know if it's really a dead body, and not just someone sleeping?

A: Dead bodies are unnaturally still, stiff, and drained of color. Also, people rarely just lie down and sleep in culverts or waist-high grass.

Q: Should I poke the dead body?

A: No, you should not.

Q: Not even with a stick?

A: Especially not with a stick!

Q: Well, what should I do, then?

A: Contact the police as soon as you can. And be prepared for reporters from local news outlets to ask to interview you.

◆ **Protect your skin.** Wear a cap or visor and sunglasses. And don't forget the sunscreen. Remember, you're dealing not just with overhead rays, but also with sun reflected off the water.

Finding Relief in Porcelain-Free Environments

In a perfect world, there would be clean, proper public toilets everywhere. They would be stocked with quilted toilet tissue, their stalls

Fig. H

would have locking doors, and an attendant would be standing by, ready to offer a hand towel and a mint. And runners would automatically go to the front of the line, if there were a line, which there never would be.

This is not a perfect world, however. Especially for runners. You therefore will very likely find yourself needing to go—sometimes urgently—in very inconvenient places. Here are some guidelines for making the most of these situations.

♦ **Off-road.** Relieving yourself behind a tree, shrub, or other natural barrier isn't ideal. But if there's nothing better around and you've really got to go, well . . . you've got to go. First, look around

Fig. 1

Q&A

Q: When I'm at the airport and see a cyclist struggling with a large bag of gear and a cumbersome hard-sided bicycle case while I just have my running shoes and some shorts stuffed into a shoulder bag, is it okay to laugh?

A: Yes.

to make sure the coast is clear. Position yourself as strategically as possible, blocking as much of your private bits as you can from as many lines of sight as possible. Continue scanning the area, back and forth, while you take care of business. But don't forget to glance down, too, just in case. [Fig. I] When you're finished, walk away nonchalantly, whistling.

+ **By the side of the road.** Also not ideal, by a long shot. Naturally, in these situations you want to get as far from the road as reasonably possible, and to stand or squat behind the largest, densest tree or shrub you can find. Beyond that, be still, make it quick, and keep an eye out for hapless bystanders.

+ **In porta potties.** As a runner, you are (or will grow to be) way more familiar with porta potties than the average citizen. You may well become a bit of a portable toilet connoisseur, debating the merits of the Tidy John versus the Honey Bucket, and mulling whether the new Johnny on the Spot model truly is an improvement over the older ones, or if the so-called upgrades are merely cosmetic. (Translucent roof? Psssh.) There's not much to tell you here, in terms of instruction: Look for the porta potty with the shortest line—no line at all usually means the porta potty in question either is locked or contains something very, very unpleasant. Once inside, check first for the presence of toilet paper, if you'll be needing some. Close the latch and get down to business. When you're finished, wash or sanitize your hands if that's an option, and be on your way. Holding the door open for the next person, with an elbow or hip, is a nice gesture.

In the most unfortunate of unfortunate cases, you may find yourself not only miles from the nearest toilet, but also miles from the nearest toilet tissue. When you badly need both. If you catch *The Runner's Field Manual*'s drift. In such instances, you may have no choice but to resort to drastic measures.

Let's put it this way: Occasionally a runner has embarked on a long run wearing two socks and returned with only one.

Quick Tip
Don't Squat Near This

And whatever you do, don't use it to wipe.

F.Y.I.

Strange but true: The sliding or rotating "occupancy" indicators found on the doors of most porta potties are not infallible. Even if one reads "Empty" or "Not In Use," someone may be in there. A quick knock and "Hello?" before entering may save you and the occupant some embarrassment.

EARN THE BADGE: TOILETRY

Requirements

(1) Name five things that may be used when toilet paper is unavailable.

(2) Demonstrate an ability to identify at least three models of portable toilets from a distance of at least 100 feet.

(3) Urinate in a public place, within 50 feet of at least three strangers, without attracting attention to yourself.

(4) Build a scale model of the human digestive system; explain the role each organ plays.

(5) Observe rows of porta potties at three separate races. Be able to predict, with 80 percent accuracy or better, which line will move the fastest. Be prepared to explain your predictions.

(6) Plot a 20-mile running route near your home. Identify at least five public rest rooms along the way, and at least five spots where you *could* go, if you really had to.

Notes

Chapter 3

Shoes, Gear & Apparel

Years ago, adults who set out to run tended to dress like boxers doing "road work." Which is to say they wore thick, gray, cotton sweats (tops and bottoms), possibly with a towel tucked into the neck of their sweatshirt for good measure.

Today we know better. Modern running clothing is highly technical, the word *technical* deriving from the Greek *teknos*, meaning "expensive."

Just a little athletic apparel humor there, readers. All kidding aside, today's technical fabrics are light-years beyond the cotton sweats of yesterday. The right running shoes, clothing, and other gear can make a huge difference in your comfort and performance.

Also, running clothes are transformative. Wearing running clothes gives us license to do things we would otherwise never do. Pee behind a shrub, for instance. Or hawk up a loogie and spit it out.

In this chapter, we'll review what you need to know, from choosing the right shoes to dressing properly for the weather, to tying a knot that won't come undone. We'll also mention the one time it's acceptable to put your running clothes in the dryer—and why.

To begin, let's get your feet wet.

Take the "Wet Test"

Not sure what type of running shoe you need? Start by looking at your feet. There are three basic foot types, each based on the height of your arches. To determine yours, take the "wet test." Here's how.

1. Pour water into a shallow pan.

2. Wet the sole of your foot.

3. Step onto a brown paper shopping bag or a blank piece of heavy, brown paper.

4. Step off and look down.

Normal (Medium) Arch

If you see about half of your arch, you have the most common foot type and are considered a normal pronator. Contrary to popular belief, pronation is a good thing. When the arch collapses inward, this "pronation" absorbs shock. As a normal pronator, you can wear just about any shoe, but you may be best suited to a stability shoe that provides moderate arch support (or medial stability). Lightweight runners with normal arches may prefer neutral-cushioned shoes without any added support, or even a performance-training shoe that offers some support but less heft, for a faster feel.

Flat (Low) Arch

If you see almost your entire footprint, you have a flat foot, which means you're probably an overpronator. That is, a microsecond after footstrike, your arch collapses inward too much, resulting in excessive foot motion and increasing your risk of injuries. You need either stability shoes or motion-control shoes. Stability shoes employ devices such as dual-density midsoles and supportive "posts" to reduce pronation; they are best for mild to moderate overpronators. Motion-control shoes have firmer support devices and are best for severe overpronators, as well as for tall, heavy (over 165 pounds), or bow-legged runners.

High Arch

If you see just your heel, the ball of your foot, and a thin line on the outside of your foot, you have a high arch—the least common foot type. This means you're likely an underpronator, or supinator, which can result in too much shock traveling up your legs, since your arch doesn't collapse enough to absorb it. Underpronators are best suited to neutral-cushioned shoes because they need a softer midsole to encourage pronation. It's vital that an underpronator's shoes have no added stability devices to reduce or control pronation, the way a stability or motion-control shoe would.

Once you're armed with this information, as always, the smartest way to ensure you get the right shoes is to seek out professional advice at a specialty running store.

The Runner's Uniform

Running male

- ◆ Sunglasses
- ◆ Shirt
- ◆ Shorts
- ◆ GPS watch
- ◆ ID bracelet
- ◆ Socks
- ◆ Shoes (optional; see "Barefoot Running: Crazy? Or Just Insane?" page 63)

Running male at rest

- ◆ Cotton baseball cap (with running logo)
- ◆ Cotton race T-shirt
- ◆ Boston Marathon jacket
- ◆ Running watch
- ◆ Jeans
- ◆ "Retired" running shoes

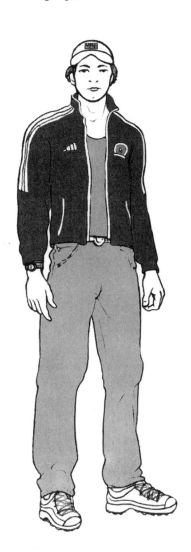

The Runner's Uniform

Running female

- Visor or cap
- Sports bra
- Shorts (or running skirt)
- Running watch
- Socks
- Shoes
- Shoelace ID tag

Optional—Both genders

- Hydration pack
- Fuel belt
- Waist pack
- Shoelace pouch

Running female at rest

- Cotton race T-shirt
- Fleece pullover
- Running watch
- Black yoga pants
- Sporty clogs

The Multilayered Runner

You've probably heard it before, but it bears repeating: When the weather is cold, wearing multiple, thinner layers of clothing is always better than wearing a single, heavy item. This is especially true if it's also wet and/or windy, and if weather conditions are liable to change during the course of your run.

For instance: Rather than wearing a short-sleeve shirt and a thick, insulated jacket for a cold-weather run, go for a thin, long-sleeve technical shirt, then perhaps a midweight fleece vest, and finally a breathable outer shell with a full-length zipper. This option gives you much more flexibility, as your clothes act as a sort of thermostat—you can zip or unzip the jacket as needed, or even remove one or more layers.

Wrap a Jacket

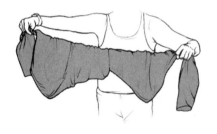

If things heat up and you do decide to remove a jacket during your run, the simplest way to carry it home is to wear it around your waist. (This method works nicely for long-sleeve shirts, too.) Here's how.

Step 1: Remove the jacket and, grasping the ends of the sleeves, flip it around and around itself to form a narrow band.

Step 2: Wrap the jacket around your waist, pull snug, and gently knot.

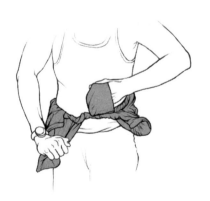

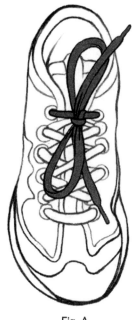

Fig. A

Fig. B

The Reef Knot:
The Only Knot a Runner Needs to Know

Many runners tie their shoes wrong. Do you?

Look down at your laces. If the bow is twisting badly to one side [Fig. A], you're probably tying your shoes using a granny knot. Many of us learned to tie a granny knot when we were first taught to tie our shoes, and we've stuck with it.

If, on the other hand, the bow of your laces is lying straight across your shoe [Fig. B], you're probably using a reef knot. Good for you! Reef knots are stronger and less likely to come undone.

We could try to describe how to tie a proper reef knot here, but it would be much easier to *show* you how. To watch a video demonstrating proper reef-knot techniques, visit runnersworld.com/shoelaces.

Q&A

Q: These shoes look really cool, and they're on sale. Should I buy them?

A: Not if those are the only two things they have going for them! Buying running shoes based solely on looks is probably the number one mistake new runners make. (And maybe a few not-so-new runners.) Buying shoes just because they're on sale may well be the number two mistake. Of course, if *the shoe that's right for you* happens to also look cool, great, go for it. And hey, if it's on sale, stock up and buy two pairs.

Shoelace Rx: "My Toes Feel Tight"

If your running shoes are crowding your toes, try using two sets of laces instead of one.

Remove your current laces and measure them. Buy two sets (four laces) half that length. On both shoes, use one lace for the bottom eyelets and a second lace for the upper eyelets. The end result will be two bows on each shoe, allowing you to tie the bottom laces looser to accommodate your wider forefoot.

Q&A

Q: How often should I replace my shoes?

A: The usual recommendation is to replace running shoes every 300 to 500 miles. Honestly, though, it varies widely, based on such factors as your weight, how efficiently you run, and even where you run. Go by feel. And if you notice unusual wear patterns on your shoes, take them with you to a specialty running store. An experienced running store salesperson can learn a lot about you and your running just by looking at your shoes.

Quick Tip

On very cold days, a plastic sandwich bag can help to keep your toes warm. Just slide it on over your sock but inside your shoe.

Caution!

Vintage Running Shoes

As a runner you may be tempted, sooner or later, to purchase a pair of "retro," vintage running shoes—not for running, but for wearing with jeans or khakis. This is an understandable urge. Many vintage running shoes look extremely cool and are comfortable. Also, vintage shoes confer a certain amount of hipness on the wearer that regular running shoes just don't. All other things being equal, a suburban dad (for example) dressed in jeans, T-shirt, and sneakers will radiate 15 percent more coolness wearing vintage running shoes than wearing a new, modern model.

Just be careful. For approximately 1 out of 10 runners, the acquisition of vintage running shoes can become a compulsion bordering on addiction. Before you know it, your closet will be overflowing with retro Adidas, Nike, and Saucony shoes, and you'll find yourself considering renting a storage unit just for your collection of vintage Onitsuka Tigers.

Please take this advice to heart. *The Runner's Field Manual* speaks from experience.

Dressing for Any Condition

Many running apparel guides use temperature ranges to suggest how much or how little clothing a runner should wear. But this fails to take into account personal "thermostats" and tolerances, windchill, and acclimatization.

Here is a more practical guide, based instead on what *non*running clothing you might wear in various conditions.

IF YOU WOULD WEAR THIS WHEN *NOT* RUNNING . . .	WEAR THIS WHEN YOU *DO* RUN*
Shorts and T-shirt	Shorts and short-sleeve shirt or tank
Jeans or pants, long-sleeve or short-sleeve shirt	Shorts and short-sleeve shirt
Jeans or pants, shirt, light jacket, possibly gloves	Shorts and long-sleeve shirt
Jeans or pants, shirt, insulated vest, gloves, possibly hat	Tights or pants, long-sleeve shirt, possibly hat and gloves
Jeans or pants, shirt, midweight coat, gloves, hat	Tights or pants, long-sleeve shirt, vest or jacket, hat, gloves
Jeans or pants, shirt, sweater, winter coat, gloves, hat, scarf	Tights or pants, long-sleeve shirt(s), jacket, hat, mittens with glove liners, wind briefs (for men), possibly neck gaiter or balaclava
Wool pants, long underwear, shirt(s), sweater, vest, parka, heavy knit hat, hood, ski goggles, scarf, Arctic-expedition-grade mittens with silk glove liners	Honestly, you probably shouldn't be out running in these conditions.

*When racing, you will feel warmer than you would on a training run, so you may want to follow clothing recommendations that are "one level above" those indicated here.

A Note on Wearing Shorts Year-Round

Guidelines and advice aside, some runners prefer to wear shorts (rather than pants or tights) year-round or nearly year-round, even in very cold climates. This is fine, if it's what you prefer. Just use a little common sense. Even die-hard shorts wearers opt for pants or tights when temperatures drop *really* low, or when very cold temps combine with rain, raising the threat of hypothermia or frostbite. And remember that a layer of petroleum jelly can help to protect bare legs in wet or cold weather.

D.I.Y.

Disposable Arm Warmers

Tube socks, those favorites of suburban dads everywhere, may not be fashionable. But with a few snips, they make great improvised arm warmers. (Tube socks are cheap, too, so you won't feel guilty about chucking your arm warmers during a race.) Simply cut the toes off a pair of socks, then pull them up over your arms.

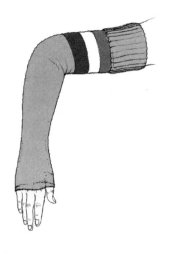

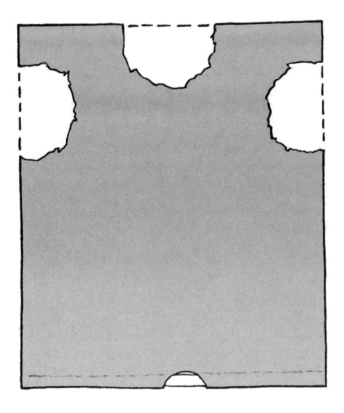

Trash Bag Poncho

Race-morning weather colder and/or wetter than you expected? The tried-and-true trash bag poncho is a low-budget solution.

Step 1: Acquire large trash bag.

Step 2: Cut or tear holes for arms and head, as shown.*

Step 3: Wear.

*Decorative flourishes—e.g., glued-on rhinestones—optional.

Q&A

Q: Are arm warmers here to stay? Or are they just a fad?

A: Good question. *The Runner's Field Manual* suspects there may be some element of fad to them; any piece of gear that appears and spreads as suddenly as arm warmers have seems likely to disappear just as quickly. But you know, they are a pretty practical option when you're running or racing in weather that's wavering between chilly and cold.

F.Y.I.

A *balaclava* is a knit cap designed to cover the neck, head, and (often) chin and mouth in very cold weather. *Baklava* is a sweet Turkish pastry made with nuts and honey. Both items are good, but you never want to get one when you really wanted the other.

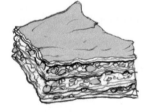

Q&A

Q: Should I use underwear with my running shorts?

A: That is an extremely personal question. Many runners scoff at the very notion, pointing out that running shorts have built-in liners, and that underwear would therefore be redundant. Many other runners—mostly men, for reasons that should be obvious—wouldn't think of wearing shorts, even with liners, without first pulling on some synthetic briefs or trunks for extra support. The short answer: The only one who can answer this question for you is *you*. Experiment and decide for yourself.

Barefoot Running: Crazy? Or Just Insane?

Okay, *The Runner's Field Manual* is having a little fun with that headline. Only because—in *The Runner's Field Manual*'s experience—barefoot enthusiasts tend to get prickly when anyone questions the wisdom of running without shoes. And *The Runner's Field Manual* finds it hard to resist pushing people's buttons.

All kidding aside, barefoot runners have always been around. For starters, there's Zola Budd, the South African who famously trained and raced barefoot; and Abebe Bikila, who won the 1960 Olympic Marathon gold medal while running barefoot.

Barefoot running has consistently attracted a relative handful of other, less-famous runners, as well. For many years, these runners existed on the sport's fringes, enjoying (or at least seeming to enjoy) a status as oddballs and outsiders.

In recent years, however, barefoot and "minimalist" running have taken off, winning over many mainstream runners. This is due in large part to Christopher McDougall's 2009 book *Born to Run*, which examined Mexico's Tarahumara Indians, who grow up running long distances over challenging terrain in bare feet or with extremely minimal "shoes."

Barefooting proponents run the gamut, from the Casually Curious ("Sounds cool; I'd like to try that") to the Evangelically Extreme ("Barefoot running cured my baldness!"). To hear some barefoot runners tell it, shoes are so crippling it's a wonder that any shoe-wearing runners are left standing. Running shoes, you suspect they're thinking, should probably be banned—or at the very least, regulated like cigarettes and not sold to minors.

Do running shoes cause more problems than they solve, or do most folks need *some* sort of shoe? Is barefoot running a "silver bullet" that could eradicate or greatly reduce running injuries, or a passing fad? *The Runner's Field Manual* doesn't know, and won't pretend

---

Quick Tip
Detecting a Running Snob

Want to tell instantly whether a specialty running store employee is a running snob? Tell him you're training for a "10-K marathon" and need a pair of shoes. If he helpfully and quietly explains that a 10-K race is 10 kilometers long and a marathon is a race of 26.2 miles, and then shows you a few shoes that might work, he's a good egg. If he snorts in derision and disappears into the back to "check on something," he's a snob. And if he hollers to the entire store, "Hey! Get a load of the 10-K marathoner over here!" he's a jerk.

Quick Tip

Just Get Dressed

Simply putting on your running clothes is an easy way to motivate yourself to actually run. Why? Because otherwise, you feel ridiculous standing around in running clothes but not running.

---

to. Maybe someday the scientific, medical, and running communities will reach some consensus on the matter.

In the meantime, here is some commonsense advice for anyone curious about barefoot running.

- Find runners who are already running barefoot and enjoying it, and ask them for pointers. (RunnersWorld.com's forums are a good place to start.)

- If you want to try barefoot or minimalist running, introduce it into your routine very gradually. Begin with, say, a single barefoot run per week, as short as a half mile, and go from there.

- Listen to your body. If it's telling you to back off a bit, back off a bit. Allow your muscles, joints, and soles—and your form—time to adapt.

- Watch out for dog doo.

And for everyone, regardless of your interest in barefooting: Mounting evidence suggests that you should run in as little shoe as possible. Any model that's more shoe than you need may well give you trouble. The staff at any good running specialty store can help guide you.

Finally, with shoes or without: Relax. Have fun.

Shoes and Gear: Care Instructions

Unless you run exclusively indoors, sooner or later your running shoes are bound to get dirty or muddy. Whether you bother to clean them is entirely up to you.

If you do decide to spruce up your shoes, you have two options.

1. Let the mud dry, then remove as much as you can with an old toothbrush; dampen a soft cloth and remove all remaining dirt, replacing or rinsing the towel as needed; wipe the exterior with a wet towel and a few drops of dish soap; remove all excess soap with another damp cloth; dry with a clean towel.

or

2. Toss 'em into the washing machine.

Seriously. It might seem crazy, but putting your running shoes in the washer every now and then really is okay. Water won't hurt them; your shoes' only true enemy is intense heat. (Translation: *Do not* put them in the dryer.)

So throw those shoes in with a load of jeans or something, select a cold/cold wash and rinse cycle, then remove them and let them air-dry. See below for more on that.

Drying Out Wet Shoes

1. Remove the insoles.

2. Towel off as much moisture as you can.

3. Stuff each shoe with crumpled-up newspaper. (*The Runner's Field Manual* prefers the *New York Times*. But that's just us.) Place out of direct sunlight, preferably in a warm, well-ventilated place.

4. After an hour or two, remove the wet newspaper and replace with dry.

5. Repeat step 4 until shoes are dry.

Washing and Drying Technical Running Apparel

More often than not, the word *technical* means, simply, "polyester." Or its functional equivalent. (In fairness, wool and wool blends have gained popularity in recent years as well.) Regardless of the exact composition of the material, your safest bet with running shorts, shirts, pants, jackets, socks, and hats is to wash gently in warm or cold water and air-dry. Drying them in a machine—even at relatively low temperatures—may reduce the life-span of your stuff.

Q&A

Q: Is it okay to wear a Boston Marathon jacket if I've never run Boston?

A: No.

(A minor, occasional exception: You may find it nice to toss your running clothes in the dryer, on low, for a few minutes immediately before dressing for a cold winter run. Doing so can make the first few minutes outdoors a bit more bearable, until you can generate your own warmth.)

D.I.Y.

Organize Your Stuff

Running may be a relatively simple sport, but do it long enough and you accumulate a lot of crap. And the more crap you have, the harder it becomes to find the particular piece of crap you're looking for. Here are a few ways to keep your running gear neat and organized.

Keep it separate. Store all your running stuff together, apart from your everyday, nonrunning things. Plastic tubs work well for this. If space is limited, look for the long, shallow kind that slides under a bed.

Subdivide it. Use smaller boxes—cardboard is fine—inside your plastic tub to further organize your stuff. One can hold socks, balled in pairs; another, short-sleeve shirts and singlets; another, shorts; and so on.

Hang it up. Over-the-door hanging shoe organizers are a neat, space-saving way to keep not just your running shoes handy, but other running gear as well—from socks and caps to rolled-up shirts and shorts to energy gels and sunglasses.

Bag it. A mesh laundry bag can help keep your running stuff separate while you wash it: Just toss the whole bag into the washing machine along with your normal laundry; when it's done, set it aside to air-dry the contents.

EARN THE BADGE: Apparel and Gear

Requirements

① Show an ability to change from pajamas into full running gear in the dark, without waking your significant other.

② Remove a long-sleeve shirt, then put it back on, while running, without stumbling or running into a tree.

③ Define the word *wicking* and explain why it's important.

④ Use electrical tape, Sharpies, and/or paint to write your name or a slogan on a technical running shirt.

⑤ Write an essay for or against the use of underwear with running shorts; use data and the historical record to defend your arguments.

⑥ Design your own running jacket, pointing out and explaining its features, colors, and materials.

Notes

Chapter 4

Foraging & Sustenance

Nutritionists and health writers are fond of saying that food is fuel, likening it to gasoline for a car. *The Runner's Field Manual* knows what they're getting at—food does fairly literally power your running—but we respectfully consider this a poor analogy.

Why? Because viewing food primarily as a fuel source, or the functional equivalent of kerosene or wood pellets, seems like a surefire way to blunt your appreciation for food. And *The Runner's Field Manual* believes that appreciating food is one of life's chief pleasures. Even if that food, occasionally, is inefficient "fuel." Or not packed with, say, phytochemicals or omega-3 fatty acids or fiber.

Of course, an overall healthy diet is important, not just for good running but for good living. *The Runner's Field Manual* endorses an overall healthy diet. *The Field Manual* also endorses the occasional cheeseburger. With the occasional side of occasional onion rings.

Therefore, this chapter will focus not just on the usual, nutritional suspects of the runner's diet, but also on things like ice cream and beer. Dig in.

Nutrients, and How to Recognize Them

Fat, carbohydrates, and protein are the main nutrients that we rely on to run. (And to jump, and swim, and just live, for that matter.)

Fat is a source of energy and is important for the absorption of fat-soluble vitamins. Fat tastes good. One gram of fat carries about 9 calories.

Carbohydrates are our primary source of energy. Carbs come in many shapes, such as bow tie, penne, and fettuccine. One gram of carbs carries about 5 calories.

Protein helps to grow and repair muscle and other tissue. It comes in the form of free-range chicken breasts. One gram of protein carries about 5 calories.

Water is so fundamental to human health that it is often not considered a nutrient at all. But it is. Also, water is particularly crucial for certain activities, such as swimming and diving. Water is calorie free.

Of course, no discussion of nutrients would be complete without including vitamins and minerals. This discussion was never intended to be complete, however, so let's move on.

Supermarket Survival

For a runner, trips to the supermarket can be very good things or very bad from a nutritional, emotional, and/or fiscal point of view. Here are some pointers.

Eat before you go. This means no shopping on the drive home from a long run or a race, when you'll be tired, smelly, and—worst of all— so famished you'll wind up eating half the stuff in your cart before you even reach the checkout, and you'll instantly regret eating most of it. Shop on a full stomach, and you'll make smarter choices.

Take a list. And stick to it. (Related to the above: Eat before you write your list!)

Read labels. Sounds obvious, but how often do you really do it? Tip: Pay particular attention to serving sizes, which marketers manipulate to fudge calorie counts.

Mmmm, Fudge. See? You're hungry, aren't you? This is exactly what *The Runner's Field Manual* was talking about.

Use a basket, not a cart. Unless you truly have a very long list and know you'll need a cart. Push a big, empty cart up and down the aisles, and stuff you don't want or need will practically leap off the shelves to fill it.

The Runner's Food Pyramid

The federal government's classic food pyramid is fine, as far as it goes. Runners may find they need to tweak its structure just a bit, though, to better fit their unique dietary needs.

Doughnuts: Use sparingly.

Gels and Chews: Use only as needed, during runs or races.

Bars: Aim for one to three servings per week from the bar group.

Pasta: Two to four servings per week; more in the week before a long run or race.

Pancakes/Waffles: Two or three servings per week, preferably after long runs. Bacon optional.

Oatmeal: Four to eight servings per week.

Beer: *The Field Manual* has no serving recommendations for the beer group. Use your head.

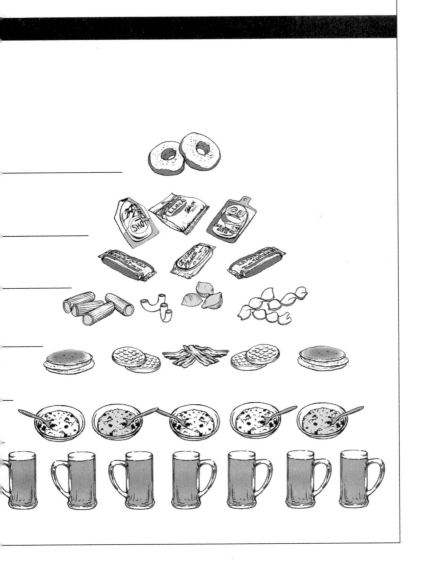

The Runner's Shopping List

A section-by-section breakdown of smart picks.

Produce

Let's face it. Just about everything in the produce department is a smart bet, except for those mysterious, spongy "dessert cups" they display next to the strawberries.

Meat

☐ Fish, such as snapper, cod, sole, and salmon.

☐ Lean cuts of meat (e.g., sirloin tip steak) with the fat trimmed.

☐ Skinless chicken breasts.

☐ Lean ground beef.

Dairy

☐ Fat-free or low-fat milk.

☐ Yogurt. Try the plain (unflavored) kind
and add your own berries.

☐ Kefir, a cultured dairy drink containing probiotics.

☐ Low-fat or fat-free cheeses and cottage cheese.

☐ Eggs. Perfect little packages of nutrients, including protein.

Frozen Foods

☐ Frozen peas. For use as an emergency ice pack to treat a sore tendon or muscle. In a pinch, you can even eat them.

☐ Healthy frozen burritos. And by "healthy," we mean the kind stuffed with beans, veggies, brown rice, lean meat, and a moderate amount of cheese. Check labels and opt for those with high amounts of carbs, protein, and fiber, and low amounts of fat and sodium. Ounce for ounce and dollar for dollar, you'll be hard-pressed to find a healthier, more filling convenience food.

☐ Frozen whole wheat waffles. Smear some peanut butter on for protein, add some berries, and you're good to go.

☐ Frozen blueberries, raspberries, blackberries, peaches, etc. Always good to have on hand for smoothies or for adding to cereal or oatmeal.

☐ Veggie crumbles. A great, easy meat substitute for pasta sauces, etc.

☐ Ice cream. Because what's the point of burning a ton of calories if you can't treat yourself once in a while?

Dry and Canned Goods

☐ Brown rice. Everything is healthier when it's on a bed of brown rice.

☐ Quinoa. This grain is tasty and easy to make.

☐ Oats. Skip the flavored, single-serving-packet variety, which tends to be high in sodium. Quick oats are better for you, and easy enough to make. Add whatever you like: berries, raisins, nuts, brown sugar, honey, etc.

The Runner's Shopping List *(continued)*

☐ Pasta. The whole "runners/pasta" thing is a bit overblown. Still, it never hurts to have some handy. Go for the whole wheat kind whenever possible.

☐ Beans, either canned or dried. They're high in carbs and protein and low in fat. Plus, they're cheap.

☐ Pasta sauce.

☐ Gummy bears, raisins, dried fruit. They all make fine substitutes for energy gels or chews.

Miscellaneous

☐ Sports drinks.

☐ Pretzels. Munch them before a long run (or even during, if you can manage it) for their salt.

☐ Olive oil.

☐ Peanut butter. An excellent, versatile source of protein and "good" fats.

☐ Whole grain bread. Look for at least 2 grams of fiber per serving.

☐ Cereal. Again, try for high-fiber varieties—5 grams or more per serving. If you must grab a box of sweet kid's cereal, try eating it mixed fifty-fifty with something healthier, such as toasted oats or bran flakes.

☐ Low-sugar chocolate syrup. For making postrun chocolate milk, the best recovery beverage known to man.

☐ *Runner's World* magazine. Duh!

D.I.Y.

Make Your Own Sports Drink

Combine the following ingredients, mix well, and chill:

½ cup orange juice
9 tablespoons sugar
⅜ teaspoon salt
2 liters water

Q&A

Q: Wouldn't it be much simpler just to buy a bottle of sports drink?

A: It sure would.

Restaurants: Order Smart

Eating at restaurants is fun. There are all sorts of options you would (or could) never make at home, and no dishes to wash. The downside is that restaurant menus can be nutritional minefields, full of hidden threats. Some tips:

◆ Order a tall glass of water. It will fill you up, with zero calories.

◆ Think twice about ordering anything described with these words: *deep-fried, pan-fried, batter-dipped, creamy, crispy, Alfredo, au gratin,* or *in cream sauce.* Such items tend to be very high in calories and fat. The word *death,* as in "Death by Chocolate," is usually a bad sign as well.

◆ Don't be shy about sharing an entrée. Portion sizes in American restaurants have gotten way out of control. Which is partly why many Americans' waistlines have gotten way out of control.

◆ Beware mayo, sour cream, butter, "special" sauces, etc. Skip them. Or at least ask to get them on the side.

◆ Mozzarella sticks are fried cheese. *Fried cheese.* Come on.

F.Y.I.

Fast Food

Don't let the name fool you—consuming this food will not make you fast. But you know what? Indulging in it every now and again won't kill you either. Even if you're in a pinch the day before a race and need something for lunch and the only recognizable source of food within sight is being purveyed by a clown and served by a teenager wearing a hairnet and a radio headset.

Vending Machines

More vending machines are offering things like fresh fruit—or so we hear. *The Runner's Field Manual* has yet to see one in real life. Much easier to find are vending machines stocked with the traditional vending machine items: chips, candy, gum, Hostess Sno Balls.

If such a machine is your only option, here are some comparatively smart bets:

- Twizzlers/licorice
- Animal crackers (sans icing)
- Nuts
- Pretzels
- Baked chips
- Gummy bears

Is It Edible?

What you can eat, in a survival situation, and what you cannot.

	Yes	No
Cattails	✓	
Ants	✓	
Kelp	✓	
KFC		✗
Nettles	✓	
Crickets	✓	
Dandelions	✓	

Q&A

Q: Can I eat a chain hotel's "continental breakfast" food?

A: Technically, yes, you can. But wouldn't you prefer some crickets?

Runners and Beer

In *The Runner's Field Manual*'s experience, most runners enjoy a good beer. More so than the average person, even. What's behind this phenomenon is anybody's guess—maybe scientists will study it someday—but here we are.

Assuming that you enjoy a good beer and that your enjoyment doesn't cross the line into overenjoyment, *The Runner's Field Manual*

encourages you to continue hoisting a cold one now and again. Beer does indeed offer some health benefits, after all: Dark beers contain heart-friendly compounds called flavonoids. And beer has B vitamins and chromium, which help to convert carbohydrates to energy.

Just watch your consumption, please. Don't forget that beer also contains something called "alcohol," which helps to convert mature adults into buffoons.

Carrying Gels and Chews During a Race

It's easy to carry energy gels, chews, and so forth with you when you run in cool or cold weather—those conditions usually call for a jacket, and jackets usually have pockets. But what about runs in warmer weather, when you might not have a pocket handy? Or when the pocket in your shorts isn't adequate? Here are a few ways you can carry your stash.

- **In your hat.** There's often room under a hat or baseball cap to carry a gel or two, or even a small pack of energy chews.

- **In your shorts.** If the pocket is too small, try safety-pinning an energy gel to your waistband.

- **In your glove.** If it's cool enough for gloves, try sliding your gel or chews inside the back of your glove.

- **In your hand.** This one seems obvious, but it might not occur to everyone to simply carry your gels or chews in your hand. (It's not as inconvenient as it sounds.)

- **In your fanny pack.** But you don't really run with a fanny pack ... do you?

EARN THE BADGE: NUTRITION FOR RUNNERS

Requirements

1. Correctly pronounce the following: *quinoa, gnocchi, shiitake, radicchio, kefir, acai, tilapia.*

2. Plan three prerace dinner menus that do not revolve around pasta. Show your work.

3. Name three uses for frozen berries that do not include smoothies.

4. Explain the difference between Daily Value, Recommended Daily Allowance, and Recommended Daily Intake. Then let us know, because we have absolutely no clue.

5. Keep a food diary for one week, recording everything you eat and drink. Wow! It's a lot, right?

6. Tour a slaughterhouse to see how meat is produced. Then go home and make a big pot of lentil soup.

Notes

Chapter 5

Running with Others

Many nonrunners assume that running is a solitary, isolating sport. (Understandably so, considering how deeply "the loneliness of the long-distance runner" is ingrained in our collective consciousness.) Of course, anyone who actually runs and has been at it for any length of time knows that this assumption isn't accurate. Running is really very social.

Sure, some folks tend to run alone, always or nearly always, whether by choice or necessity. But many more make it a habit to run with one or more partners—particularly for long runs. And races, by definition, are social events.

Even when you run alone, you're seldom truly alone. The briefest, most random passing encounter with a fellow runner engenders a sort of warm comradeship. And even if there's no one around for miles, you know deep down that you're part of something bigger. That you're part of a worldwide running community. Which is really a very nice feeling.

That's what this chapter is all about: the dynamics and the how-tos of running with others.

Joining a Running Club

Choosing a running club is like choosing a running shoe: You have to try a few on for size and find the one that fits you best. Because a poor choice can really rub you the wrong way.

Some running clubs are big, some are small; some are very competitive, others not at all; some may have very formal rules, while others make it up as they go along. Begin your research by talking to other runners in your area and asking what they know about local clubs. Visit the clubs' Web sites to see how they describe themselves, view some of their photos, and check out the other members. And before deciding, contact the club and ask to join them for a run or two. At that stage, you'll learn pretty quickly whether a club is right for you or not.

And by the way, going back to the shoe analogy: Just as some runners opt to go barefoot, the right running club for you might be no club at all. Which is fine, if that's what you prefer.

Greeting a Fellow Runner

How to greet fellow runners while you're running, or whether to greet them at all, is a surprisingly divisive topic. Some maintain that acknowledging a fellow runner is unnecessary or even intrusive, and that being annoyed when your own greeting goes ignored is silly. Others say that a little civility goes a long way, and a simple wave or nod or "hi" while passing another runner is just the polite thing to do.

It may not surprise you to learn that *The Runner's Field Manual* falls firmly in the camp of the latter.

Is it the most horrible thing in the world if a fellow runner doesn't return your "good morning," and instead motors on, machinelike, eyes locked like lasers onto the horizon? No.

Would the world be a slightly more pleasant place for everyone if only we could all see past our cocoons every now and then, and have the courtesy to reply to someone who waves or smiles at us? Especially considering what a tiny bit of time and effort it takes? And doubly especially if that person is a fellow member of the running community? Well, yes.

Even if you're absolutely, utterly exhausted and out of breath, you can achieve this effect with a slight wave of the hand or nod of the head. [Fig. A]

Fig. A

Personal Space

Sometimes, running very close to others is unavoidable—for example, in the opening mile or so of a very large race. At all other times, do your best to respect your fellow runners' personal space. For safety's sake and just as a matter of courtesy, keep some distance.

At right are some acceptable ranges for runner-to-runner proximity in various situations.

Note: The Runner's Field Manual does *not* recommend you carry a ruler or yardstick with you while you run, to measure said proximity. Especially while going downhill, fast.

Note, too, that these ranges do not apply to postrace hugs. Postrace hugs have their own guidelines. (See page 181.)

A Note on Drafting

Drafting is the act of tucking in behind another athlete in order to take advantage of the reduced wind resistance. It's more commonly associated with cycling and auto racing, but runners can benefit from drafting too, especially if there is a headwind and/or the pace is fast.

To make the most of this effect, the drafting runner must trail the leading runner very closely. Obviously this creates risks, most notably the risk that the drafting runner might clip the heel of the leading runner, causing a fall. There's also a risk that the drafting runner—especially if he's a stranger, and lingers too long—will irritate the leading runner so much that the leading runner will swerve or slow suddenly, to telegraph his irritation. Or simply turn around and pop the offender on the nose.

Therefore, *The Runner's Field Manual* discourages the use of drafting while running, unless the runners doing it are very experienced, and very friendly, and the area is reasonably free of traffic.

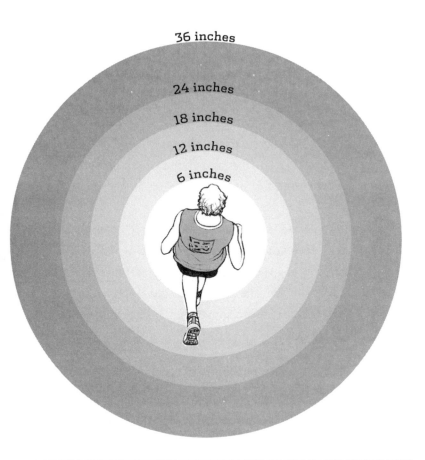

36 inches

24 inches

18 inches

12 inches

6 inches

When You Are . . .	Give Fellow Runners . . .
In the starting corral of a large race	at least 6 inches
Running in a dense pack	12 to 18 inches
Running in a thin pack	at least 18 inches
Running with one other person	at least 18 inches
Running single file against heavy traffic	24 to 36 inches
Going downhill, fast	at least 36 inches
Running at any speed on a narrow, tricky trail	at least 36 inches

The Poorly Named "Talk Test"

How do you know if you're running too hard on an easy recovery run? An oft-cited rule of thumb is to use the "talk test"—that is, your easy runs should be easy enough for you to talk with a running partner. If you can't talk, you're going too fast.

This rule would be more useful if it were named, more aptly, the "conversation test." After all, most runners can "talk" while running, even if they're running at or near race pace. They just can't talk for very long.

So, being able to gasp things like "You okay?" or "6:30, little fast" or "car back" does not mean much of anything, effortwise—you could be running at 50 percent effort level or 90 percent. Summarizing the movie you saw the previous night, complete with sound effects, however, does mean something. If you can do that, you're running pretty easy.

Running in a Group

When running with others, try to avoid situations where some of your group is running on one side of a road, while others are running on the opposite side. Such a scenario can freak drivers out, and understandably so—suddenly they have to watch for runners on two sides of the road, instead of just one. This is especially hazardous when there's traffic in both lanes; the runners essentially narrow the usable road to a dangerous degree, for drivers in both lanes. [Fig. B]

Instead, stick together as a single group [Fig. C] and try your best to move as one, crossing the road together and so on. You'll be easier for drivers to spot—and to avoid.

Fig. B

Fig. C

Running with Strangers

Never presume that another runner wants some company, or that it's okay for you to join a group of strangers for a run. Ask first. *Note:* When a lone male runner asks a lone female runner whether she'd mind if he joined her, she will almost certainly interpret it as a come-on. Even if it's not.

Running with Your Significant Other

Running with a spouse or significant other can strengthen an already-strong relationship, or wreck a weak one. Here are a few things to keep in mind.

- ◆ Be sure the distance and terrain of your run are manageable for both of you.

- ◆ The faster of the pair should remain at least half a stride behind the slower one so as not to push the pace.

- ◆ Remember: Beating your companion (e.g., to the top of a hill) is not the goal. Togetherness is.

- ◆ If your partner feels insecure about his or her appearance or athleticism, offer compliments and reassurance before, during, and after the run.

- ◆ Do not offer advice to your partner unless he or she solicits it.

- ◆ Avoid ogling other runners, pedestrians, sunbathers, etc. Uttering things like "ni-i-i-ice" or "hubba hubba" is an especially bad idea.

Quick Tip

If one member of a couple is significantly slower than the other, "runs" together are still possible; the slower of the two can accompany the faster one on a bicycle.

Running with a Baby

Pushing a jogging stroller while you run isn't exactly easy. But many running moms and dads do it, and it becomes easier with practice. It's also a wonderful way to introduce your baby to an active lifestyle early on.

If you're considering running with a baby or small child, here are some things to keep in mind.

◆ Finding a stroller that's right for you is the first step, and it's hugely important. Being stuck with a stroller that isn't comfortable for you and your child, or that doesn't perform well, or that is hard to fold and store, means you'll be much less likely to actually use it. Read as many online reviews of strollers as you can, and ask any running parents you know for recommendations. Then visit a running specialty store and see if you can test-drive a few models.

- Pay close attention to the wheels of any stroller you're considering buying. The larger the diameter of the wheels, the easier the stroller will be to push. And a front wheel that swivels, while handy for navigating tight spaces while walking, will make running with the stroller more difficult.

- When running with a stroller, try alternating your grip: Hold the stroller with your left hand while swinging your right arm as usual; after a minute or so, switch hands.

- If your stroller pulls to one side, or if you generally feel as if you're struggling to keep it pointed forward, the wheels may be out of alignment. Take it to a professional (e.g., at a bike shop) and have it adjusted.

- As with any big change to your running, gradually introduce pushing a stroller and let yourself grow accustomed to it.

- Adjust your expectations. Even the lightest jogging stroller, plus a child, amounts to a decent amount of weight. It will slow you down—especially up hills. So make peace with that fact before you start.

Note: Do not use a jogging stroller in a race unless the race in question expressly permits them, or you have cleared it first with race officials.

How NOT to Run with a Baby

- Heisman Trophy style
- Yoda-on-Luke's-back style
- Baby-duct-taped-to-your-torso style

D.I.Y.

Want to instill a love of running early on? Create a "legends of running" mobile for your baby's crib.

1. Search magazines for iconic photos of running legends; laminate and cut out four or five favorites.

2. Hang them at varying heights from metal or wooden rods.

3. Mount over baby's crib.

4. Smile as baby lies transfixed by the look of pain and triumph etched on Roger Bannister's slowly rotating face.

Foreign Runners

At some races, especially larger ones, you may encounter runners from foreign countries. (You may also encounter runners from foreign countries while traveling in foreign countries.)

Do not be alarmed. Though they may speak differently and wear slightly different-looking clothing, they are runners all the same, and therefore pretty good eggs.

Here's a quick guide to runners you might encounter from a handful of foreign countries.

NATIONALITY	IDENTIFYING CHARACTERISTICS	USEFUL PHRASE
British	Union Jack singlet; politeness; references to the queen	This is the line for the loo. (This is the line for the rest room.)
Canadian	Maple-leaf-themed clothing and/or temporary tattoos; politeness; references to hockey	Is it cold enough to need a tuque? (Is it cold enough to need a hat?)
French	French flag on singlet; baguette tucked under arm	Allez! (Go!)
Italian	Red, white, and green apparel; wild gestures while speaking	Buona fortuna! (Good luck!)
German	Red, yellow, and black apparel; strong work ethic	Ich spreche kein Deutsch. (I don't speak German.)
Mexican	Red, white, and green apparel, but not the Italian kind of red, white, and green; fluent in Spanish	¡Salud! (Cheers!/Good health!)

A Word on Trust

Do you trust your running partners? Here's a test: When you're running as a group and the runner(s) in front of you give the "all clear" to cross a road or intersection, do you double-check for yourself before crossing?

If you DO NOT look for traffic yourself before proceeding, but simply shuffle ahead, then you trust your running partners.

If you DO look for traffic yourself before proceeding, then you are smart.

Assisting Others

Whether you're racing or just running, in the city or the country, you may occasionally see someone in distress: a fellow runner doubled over, hands on knees, on the side of the road; an older woman struggling to climb some steps; a wheelchair athlete with a flat tire; and so on.

Should you pause your run and offer to help?

The short answer is "yes." No run or workout is important enough to justify ignoring a fellow human being in need.

The longer answer is "yes, usually, but it sort of depends."

If the person in question is in imminent danger or clearly ill or injured, you should assist that person ASAP, without question. If the person is merely perturbed or frustrated, or is suffering a minor inconvenience or setback, no one would expect you to interrupt your run in order to help. (Though you could still offer, of course.)

Quick Tip

See a well-worn dirt path in a front yard, running parallel to the road? Chances are good that any dog in that yard is behind an electronic fence. So you may taunt at will.

Sound subjective? It is. Just use your best judgment in these situations, and remember: It takes very little time or effort simply to *ask* whether someone is okay, or needs help.

When Strangers Ask You for Directions

Related to the above: What do you do if someone asks you for directions while you're running? The polite thing is to pause and try your best to help them out. Exceptions may be made if . . .

F.Y.I.

Use caution when stretching near others. Depending on the length of your shorts, the stretch in question, and bystanders' sight lines, you may expose certain parts of your anatomy best kept private.

- Stopping would be unsafe or highly impractical.

- You are in the middle of a workout, such as a tempo run, wherein you're breathing hard enough that you can't speak without gasping.

- The person asking for directions just does not look trustworthy, and/or is asking from deep inside a windowless van as he beckons you closer.

EARN THE BADGE: SOCIAL RUNNING

Requirements

1. Locate a running club in your area and join its members for at least two events—one as a runner, one as a volunteer.

2. Using as many runs as needed, greet 20 runners in a clear, friendly way. Chart how many return your greeting and how many do not.

3. Repeatedly invade another runner's "personal space." Record the results, including any stitches required, in a notebook.

4. Use an easy run with a friend to discuss the limitations of the talk test.

5. Plan a group run for yourself and at least three other runners. Set the meeting time and place, plan the route, and anticipate hydration needs, if any.

6. Run with your significant other, and emerge unscathed.

Notes

Chapter 6

Dealing with Motorists

Runners use public streets and roads. So do motor vehicle operators. This usually works out just fine, but it sometimes leads to friction. In this chapter, we'll outline some ways that runners can keep such friction to a minimum—by crawling into the head of the motorist. We'll compare the various kinds of motorists and the threats they can present. Also, we'll describe the safest ways to crest hills, round bends, cross streets, and more, while running in or near traffic.

Let's begin with the nuts and bolts and with a little bit of driver psychology.

Remember: CPR

All conscientious, safety-minded runners share three traits:

1. They are **conspicuous**. *Stealthy* is not a word that describes a smart runner. Stealth may work for spies, ninjas, and air force

Q&A

Q: Don't pedestrians always have the right of way?

A: Well, no. Not really. And even if they did, that "right" wouldn't stop a distracted driver from turning you into a hood ornament as you jog across a busy road. As far as *The Runner's Field Manual* is concerned, the smart runner cares more about being alive than being right.

bombers, but runners should aim to be as visible and noticeable as possible. Even if it means wearing colors normally associated with highlighters.

2. They are **predictable**. This means no sudden stops or sprints—especially across a lane of traffic. No weaving around parked cars, in and out of oncoming traffic. No veering to the left or the right without looking. Safe runners behave more or less exactly the way most reasonable drivers would expect them to.

3. They are **respectful**. Runners have every right to use public streets and roads, yes. But so do motorists, who often argue—correctly—that streets and roads were, after all, designed for vehicles. Smart runners bear this in mind. They're also mindful of the fact that a car or truck could very easily flatten them like a whole wheat tortilla—just like that. They therefore show respect and civility to the men and women operating those cars and trucks.

In short, a good runner has any of these qualities; a great runner has all three. Every time you head out the door for a run, remember: CPR. Conspicuous, predictable, respectful.

Motorists: The Frightened Rabbits of Our Roadways

It may surprise you to see drivers being compared to timid bunnies. But it's apt. Even though they may sometimes lash out at runners in what appears to be anger, and even though many of them seem oblivious or reckless, the fact is that most drivers are normal, pleasant people just trying to get from point A to point B. If they occasionally honk or scream "Get off the road!" at a runner, typically it's not because they're angry, but because they're scared. Remembering this will make your encounters with motorists much easier.

You, the runner, aren't scared. Not really. You know enough to keep a safe distance from traffic (right?) and not to needlessly put yourself in harm's way. In short, you're taking pains *not* to get clobbered by a car.

Here's the thing: Unlike most of the drivers streaming past you, you very likely have the advantage of being a runner *and* a motorist. You have the knowledge and perspective you've gained in both of those roles. Most drivers who pass you—including, we'd wager, a huge majority of the squirrelly ones—are just drivers. Running is alien to them.

So when a vehicle approaches a runner on the shoulder of the road, the runner experiences it as a normal, everyday thing and knows she is actually fairly safe; after all, hundreds if not thousands of cars have passed her before, without incident. The driver, on the other hand, sees an aberration and a potential charge of vehicular manslaughter if he isn't careful, and *why in hell do these guys have to be out here in the first place? GET OFF THE ROAD!*

In short, the driver is scared. Keep that in mind next time a motorist yells or honks: He's doing it out of fear. Not anger. So try your best to react with sympathy—not anger of your own.

The Motorist Threat Spectrum

Not all drivers are equally hazardous. Here's a look at the overall risks posed by various types of motor vehicle operators, from lowest to highest. Adjust your level of alertness accordingly.

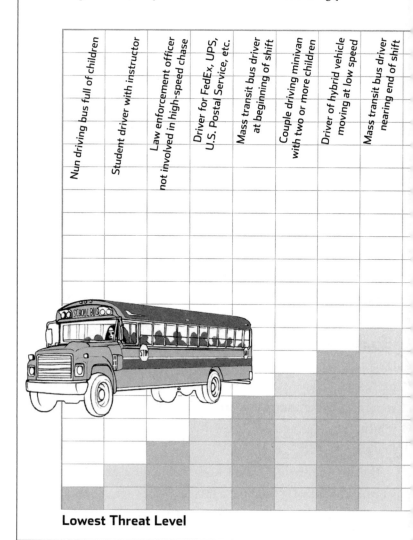

Nun driving bus full of children	Student driver with instructor	Law enforcement officer not involved in high-speed chase	Driver for FedEx, UPS, U.S. Postal Service, etc.	Mass transit bus driver at beginning of shift	Couple driving minivan with two or more children	Driver of hybrid vehicle moving at low speed	Mass transit bus driver nearing end of shift

Lowest Threat Level

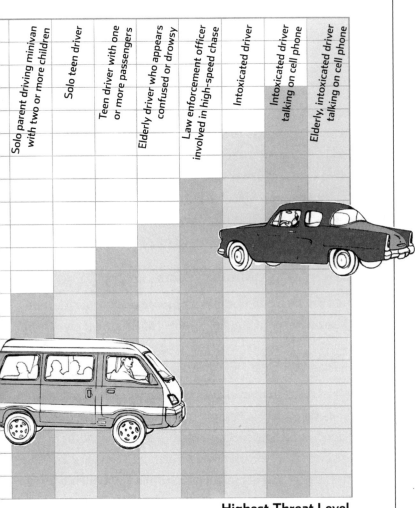

Solo parent driving minivan with two or more children	Solo teen driver	Teen driver with one or more passengers	Elderly driver who appears confused or drowsy	Law enforcement officer involved in high-speed chase	Intoxicated driver	Intoxicated driver talking on cell phone	Elderly, intoxicated driver talking on cell phone

Highest Threat Level

Quick Tip

If it's a very sunny morning or late afternoon and you're running with the sun at your back—i.e., chasing your own long shadow—be aware that oncoming drivers may have a hard time seeing you. That same bright sun is in their eyes. So be extra cautious.

Student Drivers

Many runners fear student drivers. This fear is understandable, but misplaced. If anything, a 15- or 16-year-old student driver behind the wheel of a midsize sedan is safer than the average driver. Think about it: Those kids are scared stiff of screwing up. They're hypervigilant. (You ever see a student driver on the phone?) You can be damn sure they're sober. And the instructor, sitting right next to them, *has his own brake pedal.* So stop worrying!

The "Student Driver" sign is a *good* sign.

Motorcyclists

They are not a monolithic group, so it's hard to make generalizations. Still, in the experience of *The Runner's Field Manual,* motorcyclists on average tend to be friendlier and more courteous than drivers of cars, trucks, and vans. We have a few theories as to why.

◆ By their nature, motorcyclists are much more vulnerable than drivers of other vehicles. Because they ride open and exposed, they instinctively—perhaps subconsciously—empathize with runners, who are even more exposed and vulnerable than they are. This leads to a strange sort of kinship with runners, and their behavior reflects this.

- It's much more difficult for motorcycle operators to use cell phones, PDAs, and so forth on the go. They are therefore more attentive to their surroundings, including runners, than most drivers are.

- Motorcycles simply take up much less space on the road. So it's easier for them to give a wide berth when passing runners.

For whatever reason and to whatever degree this phenomenon exists, *The Runner's Field Manual* encourages you to reinforce it. Give a friendly nod or wave to passing motorcyclists.

F.Y.I.

Some motorcyclists do tend to be more reckless than others. Rule of thumb: The more closely a motorcycle resembles a life-size version of a toy, the more reckless its operator is likely to be.

Parked Cars

You may occasionally find yourself running on a city street between oncoming traffic and a parking lane. This can be dicey, as you must simultaneously watch moving traffic and keep an eye on stationary cars that might unexpectedly pull out into your path.

It may seem safer in such situations to duck into empty parking spaces as you run, taking advantage of the "extra" room. It isn't. Instead, run predictably, maintaining as straight a line as possible—even past empty parking spots.

While you're at it, keep an eye out for drivers about to exit parked cars; they may open a door directly in your path. This isn't nearly as dangerous for runners, who run facing traffic, as it is for cyclists, who ride with it. (Cyclists who crash in such situations call it being "doored.") Still, it's something to watch out for.

Crossing Roads, Streets, Lanes, Boulevards, and Thoroughfares

Unless you live in the Arctic Circle or aboard an oceangoing vessel or you only do laps around your block, as a runner you will eventually need to cross the street or road.

This is another of those seemingly simple tasks that too many runners, too often, get wrong. Which is alarming, considering what's at stake.

On the next several pages, we'll review some common crossing scenarios and how best to manage them. *Note:* All of them assume that you are running against traffic, which should be the case nearly all the time.

Standard Right Turn

DO: Continue straight ahead, crossing to the far side of the intersection; turn right, check both ways for traffic, then run straight ahead to cross.

DON'T: As you approach the intersection, cross the street and run with traffic as you reach it; then turn right (still with traffic) before crossing again to run against traffic.

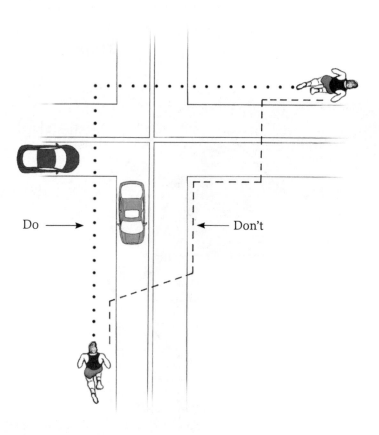

Do ⟶   ⟵ Don't

"T-Bone" Right Turn

DO: Keep running straight, beyond the intersection; turn right, check both ways for traffic, then run straight ahead to cross.

DON'T: Stop short of the intersection and cross the road, run to the turn, then cross the road again to resume running against traffic.

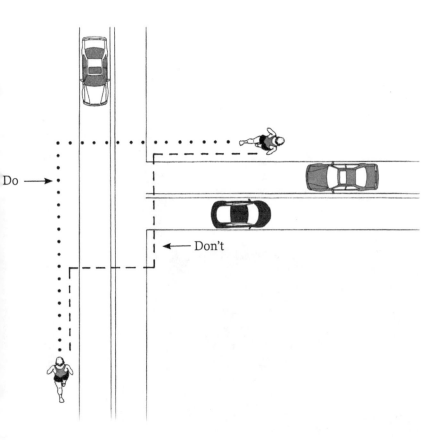

"Fork-in-the-Road" Right Turn

DO: Continue straight ahead, against traffic, until you reach the far side of the fork; check all ways for traffic, and when it's clear, quickly cross and continue against traffic.

DON'T: Cross the road before you reach the fork, running with traffic; turn right at the fork, still with traffic, then cross the road to run against traffic.

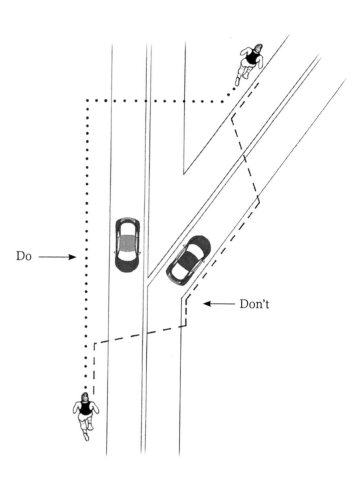

Exceptions: In rare cases, and for a variety of reasons, you may feel safer breaking the rules to run—briefly—with traffic. Here's how to cross safely in two such scenarios.

Exception # 1: If You Must Cross on a Hill (Uphill or Down)

DO: Pause at least 100 meters before the crest, look carefully for traffic in both directions, then cross as quickly as possible.

DON'T: Wait until you're just short of the crest to cross, and/or dawdle as you do so.

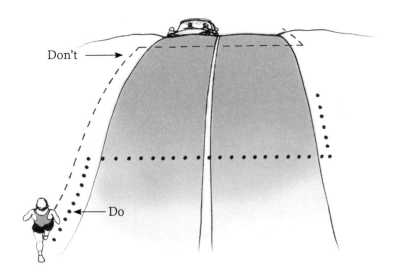

Exception # 2: If You Must Cross Near a Bend in the Road

DO: Pause at least 100 meters before the bend, look carefully for traffic in both directions, then cross as quickly as possible.

DON'T: Wait until you're just short of the bend (or in the bend itself) to cross, and/or dawdle as you do so.

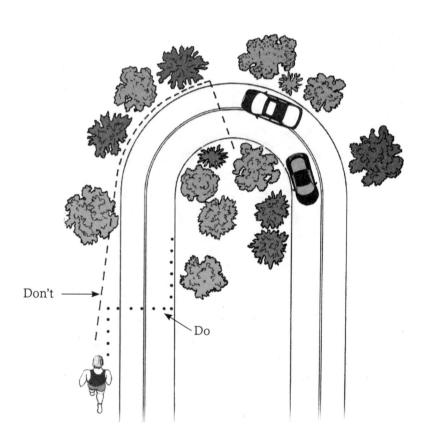

Don't

Do

Checking for Traffic

There are several methods of checking for traffic before crossing a road or street. Experiment, and use the one that works best for your temperament and patience.

- **The Tennis Match Method.** As you approach the intersection, glance left. Then right. Then left again. Then right again. Left. Right. Left. Right. Then GO! NOW! IT'S CLEAR! (Take one final left-right glance as you cross.)

- **The Once-and-Done.** Before you cross, look to your left—and keep looking, for a good three, four, or five seconds. If it's clear, you look right—again, for three, four, or five seconds. If *that* direction is clear, too, you go.

- **The One-Two-Three.** Identical to the Once-and-Done, except that you add a final, brief glance back in the original direction, as an added safeguard.

- **The 360.** The most obsessive method, this one entails checking for traffic not just to the left and right but in front of and behind you, as well. Heck, while you're at it, look up, too. You never know.

Caution!

Avoid the "Frogger" model of crossing several lanes. Be patient and wait until you have clear passage across *all lanes* of traffic, then cross all at once.

The Blind-Right-Turn Conundrum

Many drivers apparently suffer a defect that makes it impossible for them to turn their heads to the right when making a right turn. Instead, they roll up to a red light or stop sign, or a parking lot exit; flick their right-turn signal (or not); look left for traffic; then ... roll directly through their right turn. All while continuing to stare left. It's a sort of self-imposed blind spot.

Researchers are still trying to determine why this is. (Is it congenital? Some sort of spinal or neuromuscular defect? So far, they're stumped.) Meantime, as a conscientious runner who runs facing traffic, you should be extra vigilant in such situations. Assume that any driver you see who is about to make a right turn—or even any driver you *think* might be about to turn right—simply does not see you. And approach the car accordingly.

Of course, a driver in this situation will eventually see you. Typically at the very last minute, once you've stopped a few feet away, hands on hips, to let him turn. Also typically, the driver will react with alarm and may even gasp or reach for his heart as he belatedly hits the brakes.

It is not *The Runner's Field Manual*'s official stance that runners should enjoy watching clueless drivers react in this way. But you might enjoy it anyway.

Dealing with (Nonrunning) Pedestrians

Usually, pedestrians present little or no real danger to the runner. At worst, an inattentive walker might step from a curb into your path without bothering to look your way. In this respect, oddly enough, pedestrians can be a lot like drivers. Particularly if they're on the phone or diddling with an iPod. And so the safest way to approach a pedestrian is the same as the safest way to approach a motorist: Assume he or she does not see you. And behave accordingly.

One footnote (!)...Pedestrians can startle easily if you quietly approach and pass them from behind. This is especially true if you're in a relatively quiet, secluded place or if the pedestrian has zoned out. As a courtesy, try shuffling your feet loudly or coughing or even announcing "hello!" as you prepare to pass someone in such a manner. This should alert them to your presence and avert any gasps or yelps when you do pass.

The Honk Translator

A driver just honked at you. But why? What is that driver trying to say? It depends. Drivers can communicate several things with their horns, simply by changing such variables as the duration and number of honks. Here's a quick rundown.

TOOT!	"Attention! Car here!"
TOOT-TOOT!	"Hi there."/"Careful, I'm about to pass you."
TOOT-TOOT, TOO-TOO-TOOT . . . TOOT-TOOT! (a.k.a. the "Shave and a Haircut" honk)	"Hi! I know you!"
THREE OR MORE SHORT TOOTS	"I am slightly irritated, possibly because of you."
HOONNNKKK (2 to 4 seconds)	"I am definitely irritated."
HOOOOOOONNNNNNKKKKK (4 or more seconds)	"Get off the road!"
HOONNNKKK . . . HOOOOOOONNNNNNKKKKK	"GET OFF THE #&%@# ROAD!"
TOOT-TOOT-TOOT! HOONNNKKK, HOONNNKKK, HOONNNKKK! TOOT-TOOT-TOOT!	"I am in distress; send help!"

Dealing with Bicyclists

Bicyclists and runners share a peculiar relationship.

On one hand, both groups have a lot in common—cyclists and runners both share a passion for aerobic fitness and fresh air; both wear brightly colored technical clothing; both willingly ingest foodlike "gels." Most important, both groups have to share public roads with sometimes-hostile drivers.

Yet cyclists and runners can sometimes clash, which is unfortunate. It's unclear why, exactly, two groups so similar shouldn't coexist more peacefully. Maybe it's because we're all sharing a finite amount of shoulder and/or road and are understandably anxious about getting clipped. Or because, to a cyclist, a runner is just another pedestrian—an obstacle to be avoided—whereas, to a runner, a cyclist is just another vehicle coming at them, passing a wee bit too fast, too close. (And what's the deal with so many cyclists not returning a simple greeting, anyway?)

Whatever the reasons, *The Runner's Field Manual* urges all runners to treat our two-wheeled brothers and sisters with courtesy, respect, and plenty of room to pass. And to keep those simple greetings coming, even if they do go unreturned.

Running over Hills

For the road runner, it's seldom a good idea to run in or near the center of a lane. When you're running up a hill, it's a very, very bad idea. The reason for this is very simple: The closer you are to the top of a hill, the less time a driver cresting that hill has to see you. And the farther you are from the shoulder, the less room that driver has to avoid you.

So, use extra caution when running up and over hills. Stay as far to the side as safely possible. And expect the unexpected.

The Curse of the Overly Courteous Driver

It might seem ungracious to criticize anyone, ever, for being *too* courteous. But when the person in question is driving a 2-ton vehicle amid other persons driving 2-ton vehicles, and the courtesy in question actually puts everyone at risk, everything changes.

We're talking here about the well-meaning driver who is deferential to a fault. Here's an example.

You approach an intersection, running north. The light is red, so you stop and wait. The westbound driver to your right, however, who has the green light, decides to slow and wave you across the street. Through the red light. Across not just his lane of westbound traffic, but the eastbound lane, too. Despite the fact that he has the right of way, and there are (or may be) other vehicles behind him who rightfully expect him to be moving through that green light. And despite the fact that there are (or may be) vehicles in the opposing lane, motoring eastward, who may or may not notice that this driver has stopped and may or may not realize what he's trying to do.

See what we mean? This driver's heart is in the right place. But he's heightening the risk of an accident. Traffic rules and laws exist, in part, to make everyone's behavior as predictable as possible—to create a standard, shared system that dictates who does what, when, and where. When an individual unilaterally opts to flout one or more of these rules for the sake of being "nice," it's hazardous for everyone.

The Runner's Field Manual recognizes that such people are only trying to offer a kind gesture. But we wish they would just follow the rules, and find some other way to be nice.

Our advice: When you encounter one of these overly courteous drivers, make eye contact but politely decline whatever deference they're trying to offer. Shake your head while mouthing the words "No, thanks." Stay put. Smile and motion them to go on ahead. And remain there until they do. We'll all be safer.

Positive Reactions from Motorists

On rare occasions, a driver may give you some sort of positive feedback— a smile, a friendly wave, a thumbs-up, a little salute, a peace sign. Do not be alarmed. This just means that the driver in question—very possibly a fellow runner—wants to express his or her encouragement.

The proper response in these situations is simply to acknowledge the friendly gesture and return it.

EARN THE BADGE: TRAFFIC SURVIVAL

Requirements

1. Using specific examples, explain what it means that safety-minded runners are conspicuous, predictable, and respectful.

2. Arrange the following in order of threat level, from lowest to highest: intoxicated driver, hybrid vehicle moving at low speed, elderly driver who appears confused or drowsy, solo teen driver.

3. Use your own car horn to communicate the following messages: "Attention! Car here!" ... "Get off the road!" ... "Hi! I know you!"

4. Write a letter to the editor of your local newspaper, urging motorists to watch out for runners and making a case for "sharing the road."

5. Recite from memory the right and wrong way to cross the road in at least three commonly seen intersections/settings.

6. Play "Frogger" for at least 15 consecutive minutes without being crushed or drowned.

Notes

Chapter 7

Health, Safety & First Aid

Running is generally a health-promoting activity, if you take care of yourself. Knowing how to cope when something goes awry—and, more important, how to prevent something from going awry in the first place—is one of the most important skills a runner can have.

This chapter covers a wide range of health topics, from chafing to blisters, from sunscreen to toenail maintenance, and much more. We'll also discuss stretching, massage, and the importance of a good night's sleep.

But first things first. Let's take our shirts off.

Bloody Nipples

Perhaps no ailment is better known among runners than the bloody nipple, which, come to think of it, would be a terrific name for a drink. (Maybe something with cherry soda and rye whiskey?)

Bloody nipples are a common sight at any full or half-marathon. Or, more rarely, at races of shorter distances. More specifically, we should say that bloody *shirts* are a common sight at such events. The usual pattern: dual streaks of dark red, starting in the area of the nipples and going down the front of the shirt. [Fig. A]

The blood, of course, results from chafing—over time and with enough

Fig. A

repeated movement, a shirt can rub the nipple raw.

Once your nipples are chafed, there's little to do but treat them with lotion or petroleum jelly and try not to touch them. (Showers will be painful until they heal.) Better to prevent them in the first

---

F.Y.I.

If you see blood on your shirt but your nipples feel fine, you may have been hit with a stray bullet during your run. When you get home, schedule a checkup with your physician.

Q&A

Q: I'm always reading that I should "listen to my body." What the heck does that mean?

A: This means that many people tend to worry too much about when they should run, when they should stop, what to eat, how much to eat, etc., when honestly they'll be fine if they just pay attention to the body's own cues. Our bodies are remarkably good at "telling" us things relating to physical activity, nutrition, hunger, and so on. All we have to do is listen.

The trick, of course, is to learn the difference between your body saying, "Let's not run today," and your brain telling you the same thing. If you receive this message when the alarm goes off at 6 a.m. and there's a cold rain pelting your bedroom window, it's probably just your brain. Sorry. Throw back the covers and get out there.

place. You can do this with a preemptive layer of petroleum jelly or a specially produced lube, such as Body Glide. Better yet, cover your nipples with Band-Aids. (Some runners swear by duct tape instead.)

Petroleum Jelly, the Runner's Best Friend

No runner's medicine cabinet or gym bag should be without a jar of petroleum jelly. Preventing bloody nipples is just one of many uses you'll find for the stuff. Much like motor oil for your car, it lubricates and protects moving parts. You can also use it to . . .

- **Prevent blisters.** Rub a small amount over and between your toes and feet before putting on your socks.

- **Protect your thighs and nether regions.** Likewise, a thin layer of petroleum jelly can work wonders on your inner thighs, groin, and . . . well . . . anywhere a lot of prolonged friction might be an unpleasant thing.

- **Grease your pits.** Smear a generous amount of petroleum jelly under each arm. Even after a marathon, they'll be chafe free.

- **Weatherproof exposed skin.** A layer of petroleum jelly on your face, legs (especially knees), or other exposed bits will help protect them from the elements. This is particularly helpful when running in rain or snow.

F.Y.I.

A Note on "Toxins"

Certain people (massage therapists, fellow runners, etc.) often speak of "toxins" in the muscles after a hard workout or race, and the need to "flush them out." *The Runner's Field Manual* has always been a little dubious of this sort of talk and has never heard a satisfactory explanation of what these "toxins" are, exactly, and where massage flushes them.

Where to Lube

Before a long run or race, apply lube or petroleum jelly here:

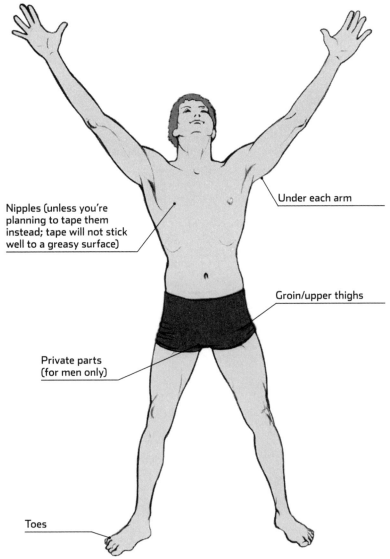

Nipples (unless you're planning to tape them instead; tape will not stick well to a greasy surface)

Under each arm

Groin/upper thighs

Private parts (for men only)

Toes

. . . And anywhere else you've experienced chafing in the past (e.g., under your waistband)

Don't Forget the Sunscreen

It's not just for the beach. Skin cancer is more common than you might think. And deadlier than you might think—particularly if it's not caught early.

In addition to regular use of sunscreen, get an annual full-body skin check by a dermatologist. And do self-checks more often, looking for any new or unusual growths or spots, as well as changes in existing ones.

Here's what to look for.

- A skin growth that increases in size and appears pearly, translucent, tan, brown, black, or multicolored
- A mole, birthmark, beauty mark, or any brown spot that:
  - changes color
  - increases in size or thickness
  - changes in texture
  - is irregular in outline
  - is bigger than 6 millimeters or ¼ inch (the size of a pencil eraser)
  - appears after age 21
- A spot or sore that continues to itch, hurt, crust, scab, erode, or bleed
- An open sore that does not heal within 3 weeks

If anything looks worrisome, have a doctor check it out.

Quick Tip

Skip the Pedicure

Pedicures are a nice way to pamper yourself. But you really want to avoid getting one before any long run or race. Why? Because the pedicurist will want to buff away calluses. And calluses, while unsightly, serve a purpose: They protect and toughen those parts of your foot that are rubbed or irritated when you run. A sudden loss of calluses means a sudden loss of that protection. That's bad news right before a long event.

Treating a Bystander Who Has Accidentally Seen Your Feet

If you've been running for more than a few months, your close friends and family members have likely adjusted to the sight of your horrible feet. Nasty blisters, funky fungus, black toenails, missing toenails, about-to-be-missing toenails ... and so on. It's nothing they haven't seen before. They don't enjoy seeing that stuff, but they've grown used to it. They have developed mental calluses in much the same way you've developed literal ones.

Strangers, however, probably have not: They are totally unprepared to catch a glimpse of your naked feet without warning. They may react with what doctors call an "acute stress reaction."

If such a thing happens, you should act fast. Here's what to do.

1. For goodness' sake, cover your feet!

2. If the person has fainted, call for help. Then make sure he is breathing and his airway is unobstructed.

3. If the person has not fainted but looks as if he might, help him to sit or lie down.

4. Instruct the person to take a series of deep breaths, inhaling and exhaling slowly and steadily.

5. Offer to get the victim a cup of water.

6. Apologize profusely. Explain that you are a runner.

How to Pop a Blister

Small blisters are best left to heal on their own. But the best way to deal with a large, painful blister is to drain it. Here's how.

Step 1: Wash and dry your hands, then clean the blister and the area around it—ideally by washing with soap and water, then swabbing with rubbing alcohol.

Step 2: Sterilize a needle or straight pin (again, with rubbing alcohol).

Q&A

Q: Do I need to take vitamin/mineral supplements?

A: Short answer? No. Longer, more nuanced answer: No, not really . . . assuming that you don't have any deficiencies or other conditions requiring supplementation, and that your diet is well balanced and includes plenty of fruits, vegetables, and grains. On the other hand, taking a daily multivitamin can't hurt, either. Your call!

Step 3: While gently squeezing the sides of the blister, pierce it with the tip of your needle.

Step 4: Drain the blister by pushing and squeezing out the fluid; dab dry with a clean cloth or tissue.

Step 5: Apply antibacterial cream and cover with an adhesive bandage.

If your blister refills with fluid, repeat the above steps. If you notice swelling, tenderness, or other troubling symptoms, see your physician.

Toenail Maintenance

If your toenails are healthy and well kept, you really should never notice them. When runners do notice their toenails, it tends to be because they are creating discomfort or pain. Or they're bleeding. Or missing. One simple step toward healthy, happy toenails is regular maintenance. Every few weeks or as needed, carefully clip your toenails after a bath or shower, when they'll be a bit softer. Cut straight across the tip of the nail [Fig. B]; clipping deeper, along the sides, can cause ingrown nails. Also, avoid clipping your toenails the night before a big race or long run. If you accidentally cut skin or clip too deep, the pain could disrupt your sleep that night—and your run the next morning.

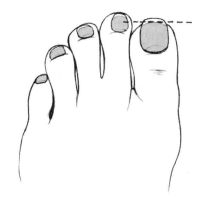

Fig. B

Personal Music Players

The Runner's Field Manual knows that this is an explosive and divisive topic. Many runners enjoy running with their iPods or other MP3 players, and some swear they couldn't run without them; others view their use, especially in races, as wrongheaded at best, and hazardous at worst. *The Field Manual* also knows that most people's minds are already made up on this matter, regardless of where they stand.

So, let us just say a few things, as matter-of-factly as we can.

- Being aware of your surroundings is the single most important thing a runner can do to run safely.

- Being aware of your surroundings is more difficult when you're listening to music through headphones or earbuds.

- Runners who use headphones while running, by definition, are rarely aware of being unaware. [Fig. C]

On another, more personal level, *The Field Manual* laments the fact

Fig. C

that so many runners, maintaining that they "need" music in order to manage, are tuning out during group runs and races. It's regrettable that running and racing is becoming that much less of a communal experience, that so many of us appear to prefer running in auditory cocoons rather than sharing every aspect of the experience with one another.

And at this point, *The Runner's Field Manual* will step off its soapbox.

Negotiating Stairs after a Marathon

For several days after you finish a marathon, tasks you once considered routine may be surprisingly difficult. Walking up and down stairs, for instance.

Here's how to cope.

◆ Take short, slow steps.

◆ If you're walking up stairs, take them one at a time.

◆ If you're descending stairs, try walking down backward. This may be noticeably easier.

◆ Wince and bear it. [Fig. D] Soon enough, you'll be back to normal.

Fig. D

Germs, Germs, Germs

Germs are everywhere. In your kitchen, your bathroom, your car. At the office and the supermarket, on the bus, in your dog's mouth. And don't even get us started on children. Kids are like walking petri dishes for germs.

Normally, germs aren't a huge deal. Stay rested and reasonably healthy, and your immune system fends off most of them. When your body is ravaged by the intensity of marathon training, however, your immune system takes a beating, too. Which means you're more vulnerable and more likely to get sick. Adding insult to injury, you're most likely to get sick when you least want to—in those final few weeks before your race, as your mileage peaks. The risk is highest, naturally, during cold and flu season.

Short of living in a plastic bubble, there are a few steps you can take to keep illness at bay in those crucial weeks before a big race.

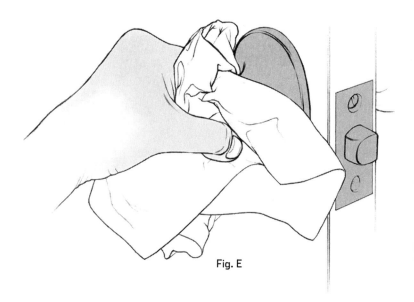

Fig. E

Wash your hands often. This is probably the single most effective thing you can do to avoid getting sick during cold and flu season. It's probably also the single most overlooked thing.

Try to open doors without your hands. Really. Especially doors in shared spaces, such as shops and public rest rooms. Instead, pull a sleeve over your fingers, or employ a napkin, tissue, or paper towel, if you have one handy. [Fig. E]

Avoid crowds. Packed restaurants, subway cars, movie theaters... you risk exposure to sick people in all of these places. This goes double for crowds with lots of small children.

Stay hydrated. Drink plenty of water. Or orange or grapefruit juice, which have the added benefit of vitamin C.

Get extra sleep whenever possible. A well-rested body is a strong body.

EARN THE BADGE: FIRST AID

Requirements

1. Acquire a blister and pop it successfully. Explain your work.
2. Using common household objects and materials from your kitchen, demonstrate how antacids work.
3. Explain the word *hyponatremia*.
4. Be able to locate and name the major muscles used in running.
5. Demonstrate proficiency with a foam roller.
6. Describe at least four ways you can protect your nipples from chafing.

Stretching

Many runners stretch. Many more do not. Whether it does any good is disputed, sometimes hotly. *The Runner's Field Manual*'s stance on stretching echoes that of *The Runner's Rule Book* (Rule 1.42). That stance is: feet shoulder-width apart, bending forward from the waist.

Sorry, couldn't resist.

No, that stance is: "If stretching seems to help you run better and feel better, then stretch. If not, then don't."

If you do decide to stretch, do so after your run or at least after warming up. Your muscles will be more pliable then. And remember: Stretch just to the point of discomfort. Pain should never enter the picture.

Here are a few basic moves.

Squat

This will stretch your back, hips, quads, and calves.

◆ Lower yourself slowly while squatting wide, keeping your knees in line with your ankles.

◆ Breathe deeply for several moments. Stand slowly. Squat one to three times.

Toe Lift

This stretches your calf muscles. Use a wall or chair to steady yourself, if necessary.

- Standing straight, shift your weight to your left leg.

- Keep your right heel on the ground and lift your right foot's toes up and back. Hold for a few seconds and release.

- Lift and release 10 times, then repeat using your left leg.

Hamstring Step

This will loosen the muscles running up and down the back of your thigh.

◆ Plant your right foot on a step, with your toes forward and knee slightly bent.

◆ Eyes ahead, lean forward from your hips.

◆ Once you feel the stretch in the hamstrings of your right leg, hold for 15 to 30 seconds. Repeat with your left leg.

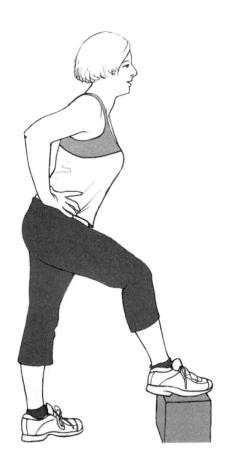

Achilles Stretch

This focuses on your Achilles tendon, which attaches your heel to your lower leg.

- Sit on the floor, with your left leg straight out; bend your right leg and pull your heel close to your butt.
- Grasp the bottom of your right foot with both hands.
- Raise the front of the foot, keeping the heel on the floor. Hold for 2 seconds; repeat 10 times with each leg.

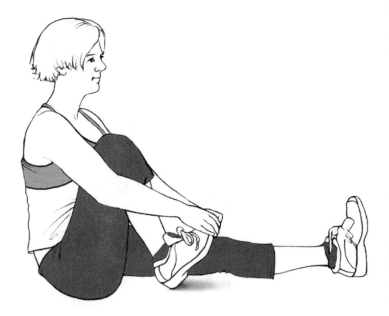

EARN THE BADGE: Stretching

Requirements

① Design a routine consisting of at least five stretches. Be prepared to explain what each stretch targets.

② Prove your ability to stretch in at least three of the following places: on an airplane; in a meeting; in line at the supermarket; in your car; at the movies; waiting at a crosswalk.

③ Write a poem based on the phrase "point of discomfort."

④ Invent a stretch of your own and name it something catchy.

⑤ Demonstrate at least three stretches that involve another runner.

⑥ Visit a health club and identify at least five mistakes you see people making as they stretch. Take notes.

The Ice Bath

As *The Runner's Rule Book* (Rule 1.20) makes clear, not everyone is sold on the benefits of sitting in an ice bath after a hard run or race. But many runners are devoted to the practice, saying that it helps to reduce muscle inflammation, speeding recovery.

Want to see for yourself? Here's how to do it.

Step 1: Dump two or three bags of ice into your tub. (If you don't have bags of ice handy, just use up whatever ice you have in the freezer.)

Step 2: Fill with enough cold water to cover you up to your waist when sitting in the tub. The water should reach between 50 and 59 degrees.

Step 3: Put on a warm hat and a jacket or sweatshirt, if you like. A warm drink might help, too.

Step 4: Ease into the water and sit there for 10 to 20 minutes.

Step 5: Hop out and put some pants on. Congratulations—you made it!

Sleep

Sleep is important. Scientists still aren't sure why, exactly. Frankly, *The Runner's Field Manual* doesn't care why. Probably you don't, either. Probably all you know is that you feel better, run better, and get sick less when you're getting good sleep most nights.

Apart from the obvious (e.g., don't chug coffee after dinner), here's how to do so.

Maintain a routine. This means going to bed at roughly the same time each night and waking up at about the same time each morning. Even on weekends.

Skip the bedtime snack. Or keep it small and eat it slowly, at least an hour before bedtime. Digesting a lot of food is a surefire route to tossing and turning.

Time your run right. Many people find it hard to fall asleep if they work out too close to bedtime. If you've been running late in the day—say, two or three hours before going to bed—and are having trouble with insomnia, experiment with running earlier until you find a pattern that works for you.

Quick Tip

The night before an early run or race, sleep in your running clothes. It will make rolling out of bed that much easier the next morning.

Plug your ears. If you've been waking up tired, experiment for a few nights with wearing earplugs to bed. Your problem may be as simple as hearing noises that are just loud enough to jolt you awake, interrupting your sleep cycle.

Limit naps. A midday catnap is a great thing, in moderation. Keep your naps to 30 minutes, max.

Bore yourself sleepy. Trying hard to fall asleep will only keep you up. So if you have trouble falling asleep, read something dull or get up and watch something boring on TV until you feel drowsy.

By the way, when you're training hard, you'll do well to grab some extra sleep. One rule of thumb says to sleep an extra minute per night for each mile per week that you train. So if you're running 40 miles per week, for instance, try your best to get an additional 40 minutes of sleep nightly that week.

Sweet dreams.

Notes

Chapter 8

Racing

Man has been racing for thousands of years. And woman has been racing for much of that time, despite the embarrassing efforts of some race directors to prevent woman from doing so, ostensibly for woman's own good. (Three cheers for Kathrine Switzer!) So our instinct to compete, to "toe the line," to "go head to head" with our fellow runners, to "see what we're made of," and possibly to "retch on the finish line," is deeply ingrained.

Entering a foot race is one of the most satisfying things a runner can do. The anticipation alone can be a real thrill. Without that carrot dangling in front of them, many runners may find it difficult to motivate themselves to get out there and run day after day, week after week.

In addition, racing provides a wonderful way to mark progress in a runner's career, especially in the early years, as personal records (PRs) are notched at various race distances. Then, of course, there is the camaraderie of the race itself, the sense of accomplishment, and the resulting boost in self-confidence. To say nothing of the free T-shirt.

In short, racing can be a valuable motivational tool for any runner, as well as a highly gratifying endeavor unto itself.

In this chapter, we'll discuss various aspects of racing, including how to find a race, tactics, aid-station strategies, celebrity encounters, and more.

Finding a Race

In bygone days, locating a race meant scanning a running club's mailed newsletter, seeing a poster in your local running specialty store, or spotting an ad in a newspaper or running publication.

Today, of course, you can search for races in and around your community—or anywhere, even overseas—online. The Race Finder tool at RunnersWorld.com is a fine resource, if *The Runner's Field Manual* does say so itself. Other valuable Web sites for finding races include MarathonGuide.com, Active.com, and CoolRunning.com.

What a Race Name Says about That Race

Note that a race with the word *shuffle, trot,* or *romp* in its name is very likely to be, for lack of a better word, fun. It is also likely to be very accommodating to newbies, costumed runners, and the "occasional," or not-so-serious, runner. This also applies to any race with a seasonal bent; words like *shamrock, Santa,* and *bunny* are tip-offs.

Conversely, a race with the word *pain, hell, mountain,* or *widowmaker* in its name is likely to be fairly hard core.

A race with the words *tot, kids,* or *pint-sized* in its title is likely to be a children's race. While adults could probably kick some serious butt in such an event, we don't advise trying to do so.

A race with the word *Olympic* in the title very probably is out of your league. Likewise, it's best to avoid these.

D.I.Y.

Buzz Your Own Hair

As noted in *The Runner's Rule Book*, buzzing your hair super short before a race can make you feel eight percent faster. Not only that, but it looks cool, too.

You could go to a barbershop or salon to have this done. Or you could buy some electric clippers and do it yourself. *The Runner's Field Manual*, which prizes frugality and resourcefulness, prefers the D.I.Y. approach.

Here's how to do it.

Step 1: Be sure your clippers are clean, then affix the proper guide. (The number 3 guide is pretty short; number 2 is very short; number 1 is extremely short.)

Step 2: Get to buzzing, sliding the clippers slowly across your scalp. On top, go from front to back; on the sides, go from bottom to top, around your ears; in the back, again, go from the bottom up. Don't press down too hard; just let the clippers glide and do their work.

Step 3: Use a mirror to spot uneven patches, and rebuzz as needed. Trimming around the ears with scissors is optional.

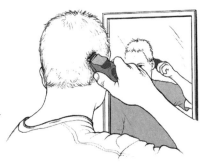

Step 4: Clean and lightly oil your clippers before putting them away, so they'll be ready for your next race!

The Race Weekend Hotel

Many a race weekend has been spoiled by a hastily selected hotel. Here are a few tips to keep in mind when making your reservation.

- You want a hotel as close to the start as reasonably possible, of course. If you're unable to find one within walking distance, consider your options carefully. Factor in the time, cost, and stress of making it from a given hotel to the start on race morning, versus the price, and choose accordingly.

- If you're torn between two comparably priced hotels, one near the start and one near the expo, take the one near the start.

- Ask for a room not too close to the ice machine or elevators.

- Most rooms today are nonsmoking by default, but it never hurts to request one when making your reservation.

  And once you're at the hotel . . .

- As soon as you can, unpack all of your running gear. If you've forgotten something important, now's the time to find out.

- Don't want to carry your room key with you when you head out for a jog, or for the race itself? Stash it somewhere in the hall (not too near your room)—under a trash can or chair, or on top of a tall vending machine. Or simply leave it with someone at the front desk.

- For peace of mind, arrange for at least two methods of waking up: Program the alarm on your cell phone and/or running watch; request a wake-up call through the front desk; set the alarm on your room's clock radio; maybe even arrange to have a friend phone you at the appropriate time.

The Runner as Roving Ambassador

When you're visiting a town or city for a race, you'll likely want to head out a day or two before the event for a short, easy run. If you do, remember that you're a very visible representative of that event, and even of the sport at large (whether you like it or not). You're also, essentially, a guest in someone else's home. So be on your very best behavior.

◆ Try not to spit or clear your nose; if you must, do it discreetly.

◆ Show extra respect to motorists.

◆ Smile and wave at pedestrians.

◆ Jog slowly on sidewalks and defer to nonrunners.

Of course, these are things you should be doing no matter where you run. But when you're a visitor in a new place, they're even more important.

Before You Fall Asleep

The less you have to worry about the night before your race, the better you'll sleep. So, before you climb into bed, do the following.

◆ Pin your bib number to the shirt or singlet you plan to wear on race day.

◆ Attach the timing band or chip to your shoe. (See page 153.)

◆ Lay out all the clothing and gear that you plan to put on the next morning, head to toe, including your watch or GPS unit.

◆ If you've brought a special food or drink for breakfast, make sure it's ready to go.

- Set out anything else you'll need in the morning, such as petroleum jelly or body lube, sunscreen, Band-Aids or nipple shields, contact lens solution, sunglasses, energy gels, etc.

- If you'll be carrying a gear-check bag to the start, prepack as much as you can. Include extra gloves, hat, and so on if there's even a tiny chance you might need them. Lean your bag against the door or hang it from your door's latch, so it will be impossible to miss on your way out.

- Review your map or directions to the start, to be sure you know where you'll be going—and about how long it will take you to get there.

- Double-check your alarm(s). As a backup, request a wake-up call for five minutes after your primary alarm is set to pop, if you haven't already.

When you're finished, take a deep breath, pull up the covers, and say a little prayer to the running gods for good weather. Sleep well!

Quick Tip
Fall Asleep Fast

Trouble falling asleep the night before your race? Just start reading the waiver you signed when you registered for it. By the time you reach the fourth use of the word *hereby*, you'll be out like a light.

How to Attach a Timing Device

Electronic timing chips, such as the ChampionChip, are small transponders used to track runners and record splits and finishing times during races. Runners secure them to their shoes, typically threading a shoelace through slots in the chip. [Fig. A]

More recently, races have used flexible plastic bands for this purpose instead. The D-tag is one popular model. Instructions for attaching the D-tag come with the tag itself, but many runners still get it wrong. That is too bad, since improper use of such tags can make them unreliable or ineffective. Two key things to remember: The D-tag must be worn on your shoe; and the tag, once assembled, must be shaped like a *D*. [Fig. B]

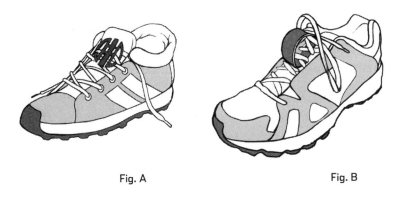

Fig. A   Fig. B

Hanky-Panky the Night Before a Race

The notion that sex before a big race will somehow hurt your performance is an old wives' tale. It's perfectly fine. Just remember to hydrate . . . and don't sprain anything important.

Q&A

Q: Should I take a shower the morning of my race?

A: If it makes you feel better, sure. Or not. If ever there was a time when the old "What's the point? I'll just get dirty again" argument applies, it's the morning of a race. On the other hand, a nice, hot shower can be an excellent way to wake up. And warm up, too— especially nice on a cold day, before heading out the door and to the start of your race.

Putting Your Name on Your Shirt

A surefire way to garner some special attention and personal support during a race is to display your name somewhere on your shirt. How you do so is up to you, of course. Just be aware that each method has its pros and cons.

Handwritten with Permanent Marker

PRO: Easy and fast; very legible if done right.

CON: Permanent marker is permanent; very cryptic if done wrong.

Bits of Electrical Tape

PRO: Mistakes are simple to fix.

CON: Some bits may peel and fall off midrace, resulting in gibberish or even inadvertent profanity.

Professional Screen Printing

PRO: Looks very . . . professional.

CON: Typos are nonrefundable; can be expensive if your name is very long.

Note: If you're running a race for a charitable cause, you may be tempted to put the name of your cause, instead of your name, on your shirt. This is fine, if you don't mind strangers shouting "Go Arthritis!" or "Yeah, M.S.!" at you.

Your Race Plan

Whether you're hoping to qualify for Boston, set a personal record, or just finish the thing, it pays to have a plan going into your race. This usually consists of two parts:

1. Having a plan.

2. Sticking to the plan.

Step 1 is a simple matter of forethought: Decide well in advance what exactly you hope to achieve on race day, and how you'll do it—e.g., what "split" you'll try to hit for each mile. Step 2 is a simple matter of discipline—e.g., trying your best to hit those splits, even if it feels like they're way too slow.

By the way, writing key splits on the back of your bib number (or even on your arm) is a good way to keep yourself honest. A company called PaceTat even sells temporary tattoos with split times for every mile of a marathon, tied to your overall time goal.

Finding the Damn Thing

Especially for smaller, local races, simply finding the starting area and the registration/bib pickup area can be a challenge. This is becoming

Q&A

Q: Should I run with a pace group during my race?

A: That depends. Pace groups—usually offered through the race itself and led by runners chosen because of their reliability—can be a nice, fun way to help you reach the finish line at or around a certain time. But some runners may find it hard to run with the same group of strangers for that long. And some pace group leaders may "motivate" their flock—usually by talking and telling stories—so incessantly (and loudly), you'll have had enough after a mile or two. Worst of all, you will find that not all pace group leaders are so reliable after all; a few have been known to take their groups through wildly fluctuating mile splits.

Still, a good pace group, under a good pace group leader, can be a real pleasure. If you're curious, try it out at your next race. If it isn't your thing, you can always leave the group and finish the race on your own.

less of a problem with the widespread use of GPS navigation systems, but it's pretty vexing when it does happen. (Not to mention stressful, particularly if you're running late and you begin to have flashbacks to those race-starting-without-you anxiety dreams.)

This is why it's always a good idea to print out a map and directions to the start the night before the race, even if you think you know where you're going.

While you're at it, jot down the cell phone number of the race director or another race official, if such information is available, before you leave home. As a last resort, you can always call for help.

If all else fails, keep your eyes peeled for other carloads of confused-looking runners, and follow them. At the very least, you can be lost together.

A Note on Parking

If you've driven to your race, it is *not* okay to speed past the official parking areas and careen through the crowds to park directly on the starting line. Even if you're very late.

The Baggage Drop

Many races offer a baggage drop, a relatively secure spot where you can check a bag (either your own or a plastic race-supplied bag) while you're racing. This is a valuable service, as it allows you to shed clothing before the start without tossing it away forever, and to stash a dry change of clothes and cab fare for after the race. Two commonsense tips:

+ Don't include anything irreplaceable or otherwise valuable in your bag. Race officials take pains (or should) to tell participants that they aren't responsible for lost or stolen goods. Rule of thumb: If losing it would make you utter one of George Carlin's "seven forbidden words," don't leave it at the baggage drop.

+ Mark your bag super clearly. Just like at the airport baggage carousel, many bags look alike. So make sure no one grabs yours by mistake.

Surviving the Start

The first half mile or so of any race tends to be chaotic. As noted in *The Runner's Rule Book*, just about every race start consists of a whole bunch of tightly packed, adrenaline-addled runners trying frantically to be in front of one another. Even if you do the wise thing and begin conservatively, patiently waiting for the crowd to thin, your safety is hardly ensured.

The popularity of MP3 players hasn't helped.

If you're trying to pass an MP3-using runner, or such a runner drifts a little too close, and you suspect that he can't hear you, simply reach out and touch his arm or elbow. This is the international gesture meant to convey "I am here, and an entanglement would end badly for both of us."

Beyond that, running in a big, dense pack of runners is a lot like running in traffic. All you can do is keep your eyes and ears open, and anticipate trouble before it happens.

F.Y.I.

Dropping into a sprinter's crouch at the start of a marathon will not gain you any sort of edge in the race, and may draw snorts of derision.

Where to Line Up

This is probably the simplest, most commonsense part of racing. It's also a part that many, many runners get wrong. With that in mind, here's a guide to lining up at the start of a large race.

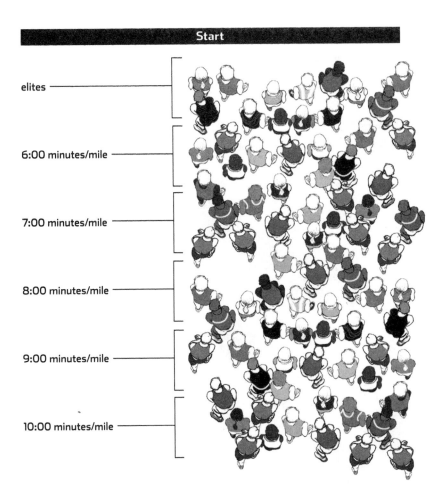

Start

elites

6:00 minutes/mile

7:00 minutes/mile

8:00 minutes/mile

9:00 minutes/mile

10:00 minutes/mile

The Clothing Toss

It's common at a cool- or cold-weather race to see runners peeling off clothing, then throwing it over everyone's heads, either just before or just after the start. The idea is to wear something old and/ or disposable while waiting for the gun, then to discard it once the race is under way.

This is a smart tactic, especially if you opted not to check a bag at the baggage drop. And there's no need to feel guilty; at most races, discarded clothing is collected and given to charity.

Just try to watch where you're tossing that jacket or T-shirt when you throw it aside. No one who gets up that early just to *watch* a race start deserves to be pegged in the face by your old, funky sweatshirt.

A high, graceful arc is the way to go. [Fig. C]

Fig. C

Q&A

Q: A friend of mine tells our nonrunning friends that she's run "a lot" of marathons. I happen to know that she has run exactly five. Is there a point at which you're entitled to tell people you've run a lot of marathons?

A: Yes. If you ever honestly can't remember, off the top of your head, exactly how many marathons you have run, congratulations: You have officially run "a lot" of marathons. If you can remember, however, just use the number.

Navigating the Aid Station

The aid station, especially at larger races, is a fascinating thing. [Fig. D, page 162] It's a living, breathing experiment in crowd dynamics, traffic control, sociology, mob mentality, Darwinism, and interpersonal communication. It can also be nerve-racking.

Here are some tips to help you get in, get hydrated, and get out... in one piece.

◆ As you approach the aid station, decide where, roughly, you'll grab your cup. If there are tables on both sides of the road, commit to one side early and focus on that one.

◆ Pass up the first few volunteers; other runners (especially newbies) will be swamping them, leaving the volunteers farther down the road relatively free.

◆ Pick a volunteer from several yards away and lock onto him; make eye contact if possible, and point at his cup.

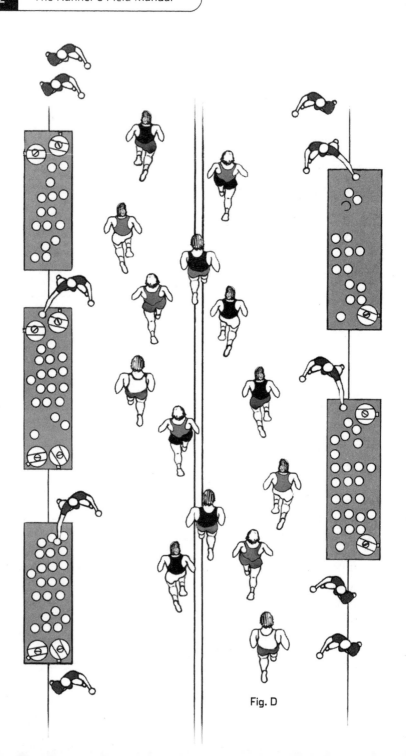

Fig. D

◆ At this point, the volunteer should be extending his cup to you. As you near it, reach out with your index finger crooked.

◆ As you grab the cup, hook your finger into it and pinch the sides. This will form a sort of spout, making it easier for you to drink. (If the cup seems too full, dump some of the contents first.)

◆ A short "thanks" to the volunteer isn't required, but it's a nice touch.

Note 1: Most aid stations offer cups of water *and* cups of sports drink. Pay attention so you know who's offering what, and grab accordingly. You don't want a mouthful of Gatorade when you're expecting water, or water when you were counting on Gatorade. And you definitely don't want to dump a cup of sports drink down the back of your neck. *The Runner's Field Manual* speaks here from experience.

Note 2: If you're going to stop or slow to a walk in order to get those fluids down, be considerate of those around you. Look around before you stop or slow, and move to one side of the road. If you don't, you just might find yourself with sports drink down the back of your neck. Someone *else's* sports drink.

Quick Tip
Shoot, Score

In most races, you'll see trash cans positioned beyond each aid station. Rather than just dropping your cup to the road, crumple it and aim for one of the cans. If you nail the shot, it'll make some volunteer's job a tiny bit easier. And you can give yourself two points!

Quick Tip

How to Race with Your Wife

For most runners, the best way to carry your wife during a race*
is by using something called the Estonian method. Here's how.

Step 1
Husband
stands facing
wife.

Step 2
Bending legs,
husband leans
forward and
puts head between
wife's knees,
clutching the
backs of
wife's thighs.

Step 3
Wife leans forward, over
husband's back, as husband
slowly straightens up, still
holding wife's legs.

Step 4
As husband rises, wife
puts arms around
husband's waist
or chest, and
holds tight.

You're ready to race!

* This tip is applicable only to those training for a wife-carrying race.**

*** Yes, there are such things. They started in Finland. It may not surprise you to hear that
beer is involved. Note that the "wife" in question need not actually be the runner's wife,
and need not be female.*

Note 3: USA Track & Field (USATF) rules say that during a race, runners may not accept fluids outside of official aid stations. So that child who hands you a Dixie cup of water from the sidewalk is, technically, helping you break the rules. The good news is that this rule really applies only to those runners in the hunt for prize money. If that doesn't describe you, don't worry about it.

Fig. E

Celebrity Encounters

Increasingly, TV and film stars, singers, and sports figures have been spotted running in marathons. [Fig. E] A particularly popular trend is for a celebrity to run for a certain cause, such as cancer research or eating-disorder awareness. Often the celebrity will be running with an entourage—unless the celebrity is Adrian Grenier, star of HBO's *Entourage,* who, oddly enough, tends to run alone.

If you see a celebrity in a race setting, do not be alarmed. Remember that stars are "regular people," just like you, except that they have a ton more money and power, and, often, enormous egos. Plus bodyguards who are former Israeli commandos.

Celebrities seldom attack without being provoked; reports of maulings in public are extremely rare. However, if you do feel threatened by a celebrity before, during, or after a race, the safest thing to do is to lie down, curl up, and remain perfectly still. The celebrity may approach you out of curiosity, but he or she will likely lose interest and walk or run away.

In short: Relax. Run your race, and let the celebrities run theirs. Just don't in any way acknowledge their presence.

Warning

Under no circumstances should you photograph celebrities during a race. They may interpret this as a threat, and have their bodyguards break your camera and/or fingers.

Spectating

The next best thing to running in a race is watching others run and cheering them on. Most runners who have raced know intuitively what makes a good spectator; for everyone else, and as a reminder for us all, here are some dos and don'ts for those standing on the sidelines.

DO	DON'T
Applaud vigorously.	Applaud in that weak, *single clap* . . . *pause* . . . *single clap* . . . *pause* . . . way. It sounds sarcastic!*
Hold up signs written in BIG, bold, clear letters.	Hold up signs written on white poster board with blue ballpoint pen. In cursive.
Use short, funny slogans on your sign, such as "Run Like Snot!"	Use slogans that are so long no runner could possibly read them, such as "Far better is it to dare mighty things, to win glorious triumphs even though checkered by failure, than to rank with those poor spirits who neither enjoy nor suffer much because they live in the gray twilight that knows neither victory nor defeat."
Tell runners that they're looking great.	Tell runners that the winner finished an hour ago.

* Exception: The weak, sarcastic clap is okay if you intend to sarcastically "congratulate" someone—for instance, a runner who has just committed a race foul. (See page 177.)

Fig. F

High-Five, but Keep It Safe

When you're racing, you don't generally have the time and energy to pause and thank all the spectators lining the road to cheer for you. But you can high-five them. This is an especially nice gesture if a spectator is already holding his hand high in anticipation of being fived by a passing runner.

It's doubly especially nice if the spectator in question is a small child. What a nice way to encourage the little one and to reinforce his interest in healthy, active living!

When high-fiving children under the age of 12, however, just use caution. A too-hard high-five may have unpleasant consequences. [Fig. F]

Quick Tip

If a spectator or volunteer is offering it via plastic tub or tongue depressor, it isn't energy gel—it's petroleum jelly. Do not ingest!

Quick Tip

Paper or Plastic?

If you're planning to hand out cups of water or sports drink while spectating, don't use rigid plastic cups; use paper ones instead. (Plastic cups create a hazard underfoot.)

EARN THE BADGE: **MARATHON SPECTATING**

Requirements

(1) Using only poster board, ballpoint pen, glue, and glitter, design a sign that can be read easily from a distance of at least 30 feet.

(2) Create your own cheer, using the name of a close friend or loved one.

(3) Find a marathon that follows an out-and-back or loop course, then plot at least four points on the course map where you could reasonably expect to spot the same runner during the race.

(4) List at least five motivational phrases that you can shout that do *not* include the words *good, great,* or *strong.*

(5) Demonstrate an ability to snap a clear photo of a runner moving at 7-minute-per-mile pace or faster.

(6) Be able to stand in the same spot for up to 2 hours at a time.

Common Displays of Finish-Line Emotion

The Raised Fist

A single raised fist signifies triumph.

The Double Raised Fists

Two raised fists = twice the triumph. (Pumping optional.)

The Upraised-Holding-Hands with Running Partner

They did it! Together! Nothing can stop them! They just might continue holding hands all the way through the chute, past the refreshments, back to their hotel, and possibly right into the shower! Yay!

The Meek, Barely Raised Palms

This one rates a feeble 2.5 on the Triumph Scale. Maybe the finisher is tired or just doesn't like to make a fuss. Whatever the reason, he cruises across the line flashing just the slightest hint of a smile, with hands raised to around chest height, palms facing front. Yay.

The No-Signs-of-Life

This guy makes the Meek, Barely Raised Palms finisher look like a raucous attention whore. Does he even realize he's finishing a race? Judging by the lack of any discernible reaction or emotion, no. You sort of expect him to yawn.

The Low-Key High-Five with Race Official

This one is a classy, understated option—celebratory without being showy. Plus, it includes a little acknowledgment of the organizers. Nice touch.

The Look of Utter Shock

Below the neck, her body language says, "I am finishing a race." The expression on her face, meanwhile, says, "HOLY &$%#! I AM FINISHING A RACE!"

The Look of Utter Exhaustion

Below the neck, his body language says, "I have absolutely zero gas left in the tank and am about to collapse like a marionette." The expression on his face, meanwhile, says exactly the same thing.

The Kneeling Ground-Kiss [Fig. G]

This one is usually reserved for the winner of the race. Though it could be used by anyone who really enjoys kissing. Or asphalt.

Fig. G

The Cartwheel

This person conserved a little too much energy during the race.

Know Your Race Courses

Point to Point: The race starts at one location and finishes at another—possibly, but not necessarily, far apart. The Boston and New York City Marathons are two notable examples of point-to-point courses.

Out and Back: The race starts in one direction, then doubles back on itself to end in the same location.

Loop: The start and finish are in the same general location, but in between, the course forms a large loop shape.

Lollipop: A blend of out-and-back and loop, the lollipop course starts and ends along the same stretch but includes a loop in the middle. So named because, seen from above, the course somewhat resembles a lollipop, with start and finish at the bottom of the stick.

Wormhole: A rare form of race course that takes runners through space and time, at unexpected intervals, via topological portals. *Note:* May interfere with chip timing.

Showboating on the Course

You may be tempted to showboat—or, to use official USATF terminology, "ham it up"—here and there during your race. *The Runner's Field Manual* not only allows for such behavior, it strongly supports it. As long as it does not occur during the singing of the national anthem.

Showboating during a race may include, but is not limited to: whooping; hollering; pumping one or both fists; making the "raise the roof" gesture; clapping; pausing to hug and/or kiss one or more spectators; any form of dancing; "double pointing" at bystanders; using a kazoo, harmonica, or other noisy instrument; conspicuously pointing to your own shirt, on which you've written your name or someone else's, or a pithy or funny or risqué message; directly addressing the crowd, especially at great volume; or, ideally, any combination of these.

Here are a few instances where a bit of showboating may be in order, and why.

WHERE	WHY
Just as the gun goes off and everyone starts moving forward.	To vent nervous energy, and to reciprocate spectators' displays of enthusiasm.
When passing by a group of attractive, young members of the opposite sex. (See also, most notably, Boston Marathon, Girls of Wellesley.)	Because using words to express your sincere appreciation for these young spectators' presence along the course, and to celebrate their attractiveness and youth and *joie de vivre*, takes up a lot of time and precious oxygen. Raising a fist and saying "woooooooo!" does not.
Any point along the course where more than a handful of spectators are outside, drinking beer from a keg.	Because . . . uh . . . PAAAARRRR-TEEEE!
During those long, lonely miles in the middle of a race where your spirits begin to flag (e.g., by holding one hand to your ear, in an exaggerated "I can't HEAR you!" fashion).	To incite a reaction among the spectators, and then to feed off that energy.
As you approach the line and realize that—barring some calamity, such as a jet engine falling from the sky and crushing you—you *are* going to finish this thing, after all.	Because people are killed so rarely by falling jet engines.

Running the Tangents

During a routine training run, you're at one corner of an empty parking lot. [Fig. H] You want to get to the opposite corner. Do you:

a. Run along one side of the lot until you reach the near corner, make a 90-degree turn, then proceed to the next corner? (Dashed line.)

b. Make a beeline for the opposite corner? (Dotted line.)

The answer, of course, is *b*. Heading directly for the corner is the fastest, most efficient way to cover that ground.

The same principle applies on race courses, where this is called "running the tangents." [Fig. I] Whenever possible, use this method on bends and turns on the course. It may sound silly, but over a long race, the time savings can add up.

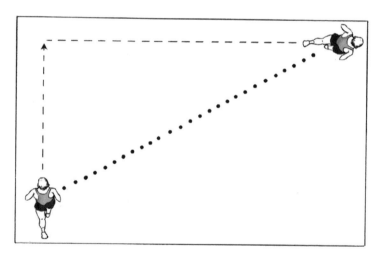

Fig. H

Q&A

Q: Can running the tangents save me time in real life, too?

A: You bet. Try it next time you're shopping at the supermarket. You may bruise a few shins with your cart, but you'll shave precious seconds off your shopping time!

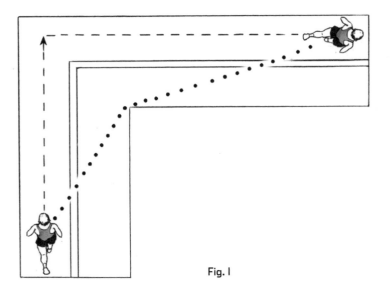

Fig. 1

Q&A

Q: What's the protocol for proposing marriage to someone during or just after a race?

A: The first rule is not to vomit on your intended, if you can help it. For this reason it's best to propose in a more casual race, where you're not really going all out. (This is why you see so few marriage proposals among, say, the elites in the Boston Marathon.) Beyond that, the etiquette is largely the same as for any other proposal: Be direct, be sweet, have the ring ready, and—on the chance that she says no—be prepared for a very awkward cooldown.

Doubling Back after the Finish

Is it rude to finish a race, collect your medal, and then jog back along the course as other runners continue to stream in? Some think so. As far as *The Runner's Field Manual* is concerned, it all depends on how you do it.

If you double back in a cocky way, with your medal in plain sight, barely even acknowledging the runners still on the course ... yeah, that's a little rude. (Great, you finished already. No need to rub it in.)

On the other hand, if you jog or walk back along the course with the intent of hooting and hollering for those still on the course, encouraging them to keep it up and congratulating them on a job well done ... well, that puts the "cool" in cooldown.

Regardless, it goes without saying that a runner who has already finished the race shouldn't be on the course itself. Shouting words of encouragement is great, but not if you're physically in the way of the person you're trying to encourage.

Race Fouls

You won't find them in any official USATF rule book—though you might find them in the very unofficial *Runner's Rule Book*—but the following practices are fouls in spirit if not by law. All of these practices are frowned upon in racing, and—depending on the severity of the offense—may earn you a poke with a sharp stick.

- Not lining up where you belong at the start

- Not removing your hat during the singing of the national anthem

- Clipping the heel of the runner in front of you

- Stopping suddenly, without warning

- Running a race you haven't registered for (i.e., banditing)

- Running with music turned up so loud, you are oblivious to everything around you

- Veering left or right across the road without looking first

- Blowing snot, spit, phlegm, or any other bodily fluid onto another runner

- Cutting in line at a porta potty

- Relieving yourself in view of others when it is avoidable

- Taking more than your share of postrace refreshments

Space Blanket Techniques

At most large races, volunteers offer finishers a Mylar "space blanket" shortly after they finish. These blankets don't look like they offer much in the way of warmth. And they don't! Still, they're better than nothing. Here are a few ways you can wear them.

Cape style. This is by far the most popular method of wearing a space blanket. You simply drape it over your shoulders (or have it draped there for you by a volunteer), then pull it together in the front with one or both hands.

Skirt style. Less common, but more stylish. A good option if your torso is relatively warm but your legs are freezing.

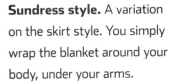

Sundress style. A variation on the skirt style. You simply wrap the blanket around your body, under your arms.

Turban style. We've never actually seen this in real life. But it sounds interesting, doesn't it?

Dealing with Finish-Line Vomit

It's a sad reality for many runners that what goes down must sometimes come up. You see this occasionally with elites. They cross the finish line, bend forward with hands on knees, and calmly spew. They have literally run till they puked. Then they wipe their mouths and smile for photos.

Even mid- and back-of-the-pack runners can succumb to this from time to time, when a hard charge to the line culminates in the tossing of one's cookies. It's not pleasant, but it happens. When it does, here's how to cope.

- **If you're the one vomiting,** or about to, first try to find a reasonably clear radius of ground. You don't want to hit bystanders, or their shoes, if you can help it. Next, lean forward slightly; assume the wide-stance, hands-on-knees pose favored by elites, if you're able. This offers stability and helps to keep the mess off your own clothing. When you're finished, try to drink something—and seek medical help ASAP if you still feel unwell in any way.

- **If you see someone vomiting,** or about to, make some room. But stand nearby, in case the victim needs assistance or begins to fall. Afterward, the best thing you can offer is empathy and help in finding a cup of water or sports drink. If a race official or medical volunteer hasn't already noticed the vomiting, find one and point it out. The victim may want or need to be checked out.

- **If you see vomit after the fact,** notify a race official so that someone can clean it up. Not only is it an unpleasant sight, it's a slip hazard. (Seriously.)

Postrace Hugs

For how long may you embrace someone after you've finished a race, without things getting weird? Use these guidelines.

Baseline Duration of Postrace Hug	3 Seconds
If the hugger personally knows the huggee	+ 2 seconds
If the hugger and the huggee are strangers	– 1 second
If the hugger knows the huggee just ran a PR	+ 2 seconds
If both parties are soaked in sweat	+ 1 second
If one party is reasonably dry and clean	– 1 second
If the hugger is male and the huggee is female	– 1 second
If the hugger is female and the huggee is male	+ 1 second
If the hugger and the huggee are a couple	+ 3 to 5 seconds
If the hugger and the huggee are a couple, but their spouses are nearby	– 2.5 seconds

The Parking Lot Wipedown

It's possible to wash up fairly well after a race, even if no showers or sinks are available. You may not achieve "Brunch at the Ritz" levels of cleanliness, but you'll at least reach "Coffee and Grand Slam at Denny's" standards.

Here's how to do it and what you'll need to do it right.

You will need:

- Antibacterial or baby wipes
- Two washcloths or hand towels
- One large bath towel or beach towel
- Bottle of water
- Large plastic bag

How to do it:

1. Standing behind an open car door for more privacy if possible, wrap a large towel high around your waist.

2. Remove your shoes; socks; and shorts, tights, or pants.

3. Dampen a washcloth or hand towel, and wipe away as much sweat and salt as you can.

4. Reaching under the towel, clean yourself with antibacterial or baby wipes.

5. Dry yourself with another washcloth or hand towel.

6. Put on dry clothes, stuffing your wet race clothing in a plastic bag.

7. Pile into the car and head for the nearest Denny's.

In her 1969 book *On Death and Dying*, the Swiss psychiatrist Elisabeth Kübler-Ross outlined a model of grieving now commonly referred to as "the five stages of grief." The Kübler-Ross model describes five distinct phases that people go through in order to cope with loss or tragedy.

Any runner who has completed a marathon—or anybody close to someone who has—may find these stages eerily familiar. You may experience some or all of these in the days and weeks after a marathon, or after any significant run for which you experienced a long, focused buildup.

With a tip of the hat to Dr. Kübler-Ross, here are the five stages of marathon grief:

1. **Denial** ("No. It can't be over. What will I do with my weekends?")

2. **Anger** ("I can't believe I missed my goal by 48 seconds. That's less than 2 seconds per mile! I couldn't run 2 seconds per mile faster?!")

3. **Bargaining** ("Lord, let my chip time be a mistake. Have the race director e-mail me to say that there was a glitch with the finish line mat and that I actually qualified for Boston, and I'll never give another reckless driver the finger ever again.")

4. **Depression** ("It's over. What will I do with my weekends?")

5. **Acceptance** ("Hey, maybe I should sign up for another marathon. One with a fast course this time.")

The Runner's Field Manual extends its gratitude to Jim Warrenfeltz for inspiring this entry.

EARN THE BADGE: RACE SURVIVAL

Requirements

1. Define the following terms, unaided: *corral, gun time, chute, point to point, chip, wall, G.I. distress.*

2. Create your own 16-week training plan from scratch. Show your work.

3. Construct a diorama showing all the parts of a typical race aid station. Explain.

4. Visit the Web site of a major race and find the following information: date of race, how to register, time and place of expo, course elevation map, past results, and how to contact race officials.

5. Describe how you would adjust your race-day plan to account for the following contingencies: upset stomach, high wind and rain, extreme heat, extreme cold, unfamiliar sports drink served on course, and hairy man in your corral dressed only in Speedo and fairy wings.

6. While running at race pace, grab a cup of water and a cup of overly sweet lemon-lime Gatorade; without slowing, dilute the Gatorade with the water until it is palatable.

Notes

Appendix & Miscellany

A Condensed and Hastily Researched History of Running

Man has been running practically from the day he could stand. [Fig. A] As such, the story of running is the story of human history itself. Space is limited here, though. So rather than get into war, politics, nation building, art, science, medicine, industry, and all those other parts of human history, let's just stick to the strictly running-related bits.

On the following pages, a timeline featuring some key dates.

Fig. A

~200,000 BC: Early humans discover that they can use running to escape predators—or to capture prey, using a technique called persistence hunting, wherein the prey is tracked and chased to exhaustion. This method of hunting would fall out of favor with the advent of agriculture and toaster pastries.

490 BC: A soldier named Pheidippides completes history's first-ever marathon when he runs from the Greek city of Marathon to Athens to raise awareness of subjugation by the Persians.

AD 14th century: Running first gains popularity as a leisure pursuit during the Renaissance. In fact, Michelangelo's sketches for the Sistine Chapel ceiling originally depict a 5-K fun run. The pope frowns on this approach, considering it vain; hence the final product. Before discovering painting, Sandro Botticelli focuses on running, culminating in a marathon PR of 2:23. (Yes, this is approximately 400 years *before* the advent of the modern marathon. They aren't called Renaissance men for nothing.)

1557: In his book *The Prophecies*, Nostradamus predicts "a great boom in running" will occur in the 20th century, in a "new world across the sea."

1896: The marathon is introduced into the Olympics. The first Olympic Marathon is just 24.85 miles, for reasons we won't bore you with. At the 1908 Olympics, the distance is pegged at 26.22 miles—also for reasons we won't bore you with—where it has been ever since.

Distance runners in the late 19th and early 20th centuries are known for their floppy haircuts, enormous shorts, and skimpy leather shoes. Also for their predilection for feasting on pork chops, hard-boiled eggs, black bread, and ale the night before a race. Distance runners in the late 19th and early 20th centuries are many things, but dietetically savvy is not one of them.

1970: An Oregon waffle enthusiast named Bill "Swoosh" Bowerman fills his wife's waffle iron with a rubber compound, irritating his wife and ruining breakfast. The upshot: He goes on to use his "waffle sole" to launch a new kind of lightweight running shoe and that shoe helps to launch a company called Blue Ribbon Sports and that company becomes Nike and Bowerman grows rich enough to take his wife out for breakfast. Every day, if he wants to.

Also, Bowerman and his shoes help to spark a running boom in America.

1977: Jim Fixx publishes the best-selling book *The Complete Book of Running,* which also helps to spark a running boom, convincing countless Americans that aerobic exercise is good for them. Then Fixx dies after a run, convincing countless Americans that aerobic exercise will kill them. Eventually, the nation reaches a middle ground, wherein many Americans run regularly, and love it, with overwhelmingly positive results; and many more Americans do not run, and grow plump, with poor results.

1984: Joan Benoit (later Joan Samuelson), an American, wins a gold medal in the first-ever Olympic Marathon for women, ushering in a running boom.

1992: Another running boom occurs when everyone least expects it, apparently spontaneously.

2009: Barefoot running captures 1.2 percent of the running community's imagination, thanks largely to the popularity of Christopher McDougall's book *Born to Run,* based on the song by Bruce Springsteen. Another running boom ensues, though this one is much quieter, on account of all those shoeless runners.

2010: Runners eagerly await the next running boom.

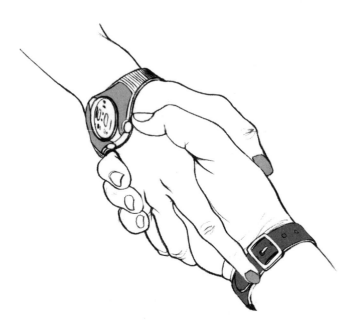

The Runner's Handshake

The "runner's handshake" may be used whenever greeting a fellow runner, as a gesture of goodwill and brotherhood. Even runners from foreign cultures are likely to understand this nonverbal way of saying, "Hello, friend."

To perform the runner's handshake, extend your hand, thumb up and fingers together and outstretched; when your fellow runner does the same, grasp his hand firmly, wrapping your fingers and thumb around his hand, then pump gently a few times.

Come to think of it, this is just a regular handshake, isn't it?

Let's move on.

Running-centric E-Mail Addresses and Usernames

Show the world how much you love running, via a running-centric e-mail address or username. It's easy. Just choose one word or phrase from column A, then add one from column B.

COLUMN A	COLUMN B
Runner	Dude
Running	Guy
Run	Chick
Love2Run	Chica
26.2	God
13.1	Goddess
Barefoot	Mom
Sole	Dad

An Unscientific Guide to Running Equivalents

60 minutes of mowing grass (self-propelled power mower)	1 mile of running
60 minutes of mowing grass (non-self-propelled power mower)	1.5 miles
30 minutes of shoveling dry, fluffy snow	3 miles
30 minutes of shoveling wet snow	5 miles
20 minutes of raking leaves	1 mile
10 minutes of scrubbing tub and/or shower stall	½ mile
10 minutes of sweeping floor and/or vacuuming	400 meters

Bumper Stickers and T-Shirts

Tell total strangers of your love for running via your car's bumper or your chest. Here are a few popular options.

RUNNING IS A
MENTAL SPORT
AND WE ARE ALL
INSANE

My Sport Is Your
Sport's Punishment

Distance Runners Do It
L O N G E R

IF I DIDN'T RUN,
I'D FEEL LIKE YOU DO.

eat   sleep   run

Got Toenails?

HELL AND BACK   26.2

Running: The Only Sport That Requires Two Balls

Trample the Weak, Hurdle the Dead

Endurance Is a Virtue

Life Is Short—
Running Makes
It Seem Longer

Who
Fartlek'd?

Run Like
a Girl

RUNNING:
Cheaper Than Therapy

Racing
B ✦ I ✦ N ✦ G ✦ O

Snot rocket (not your own)	Runner wearing garbage bag	Spelling error on spectator's sign	Jesus-related slogan on back of shirt	Beer-related slogan on back of shirt
Recognizable elite athlete	Elvis costume	Barefoot runner	Theme from *Rocky*	Theme from *Chariots of Fire*
Police officer who doesn't return your greeting	Child offering orange wedge	**FREE SPACE**	Runner peeing behind tree	"Go Mommy!" spectator sign
"Go Daddy!" spectator sign	Beer keg	The phrase "water on your left, Gatorade on your right"	Canadian flag temporary tattoo	Evidence of bloody nipples
Runner on cell phone	Runner carrying full-size flag	Bagpiper(s)	"You're almost there!"	Runner cursing upon checking a mile split

Photocopy this page and pass out copies to your running partners for your next race. Mark each square as you see or hear what's indicated there. The center is a free square. First one to fill an entire row (vertically, horizontally, or diagonally) wins!

Landmarks You Can Use for Impromptu Speed Workouts on the Road

No track? No problem. Use any of the following common objects to mark segments for a road speed session.

- Telephone poles
- Road signs
- Mailboxes

- Starbucks stores
- Passed-out vagrants
- Wide-awake vagrants

Runner-Friendly Baby Names

You're expecting a baby? Congratulations! When choosing a name, why not opt for one that connotes your love of running? A few possibilities:

- Meb
- Geb
- Seb (Sebastian)
- Pre
- Deena
- Grete
- Haile
- Joanie

- Paula
- Emil
- Bannister
- Usain
- Uta
- Alberto
- Flanagan
- Fartlek*

* Okay, just kidding. It would be kind of a fun name, though, wouldn't it?

Hobo Signs

In the decades around the Great Depression, hoboes enjoyed a sort of golden age. During this time, the traveling tramps even developed their own secret code, leaving symbols on sidewalks and streets that would alert other hoboes to a generous homeowner or a dangerous dog, etc.

These symbols, like hoboes in general, have fallen out of favor. But they could be very helpful for runners who wish to leave messages for other runners. It is *The Runner's Field Manual*'s position that we should all try to revive the use of such symbols.

Here are a few that we might find useful.

Homeowner has a gun	Get out fast, hoboes not welcome in the area
Barking dog	A nice lady lives here
Good road to follow	Good water here
No use going in this direction	A beating awaits you here

Race-Pace Chart

Time/ Mile	2 mi	5-K (3.1 mi)	4 mi	5 mi	10-K (6.2 mi)	12-K (7.46 m
5:30	11:00	17:05	22:00	27:30	34:11	41:00
5:45	11:30	17:52	23:00	28:45	35:44	42:52
6:00	12:00	18:39	24:00	30:00	37:17	44:44
6:15	12:30	19:25	25:00	31:15	38:50	46:36
6:30	13:00	20:12	26:00	32:30	40:23	48:28
6:45	13:30	20:58	27:00	33:45	41:57	50:20
7:00	14:00	21:45	28:00	35:00	43:30	52:12
7:15	14:30	22:32	29:00	36:15	45:03	54:03
7:30	15:00	23:18	30:00	37:30	46:38	55:55
7:45	15:30	24:05	31:00	38:45	48:10	57:47
8:00	16:00	24:51	32:00	40:00	49:43	59:39
8:15	16:30	25:38	33:00	41:15	51:16	1:01:31
8:30	17:00	26:25	34:00	42:30	52:49	1:03:23
8:45	17:30	27:11	35:00	43:45	54:22	1:05:14
9:00	18:00	27:58	36:00	45:00	55:56	1:07:06
9:15	18:30	28:44	37:00	46:15	57:29	1:08:58
9:30	19:00	29:31	38:00	47:30	59:02	1:10:50
9:45	19:30	30:18	39:00	48:45	1:00:35	1:12:42
10:00	20:00	31:04	40:00	50:00	1:02:08	1:14:34
10:30	21:00	32:37	42:00	52:30	1:05:15	1:18:17
11:00	22:00	34:11	44:00	55:00	1:08:21	1:22:01
11:30	23:00	35:44	46:00	57:30	1:11:28	1:25:45
12:00	24:00	37:17	48:00	1:00:00	1:14:34	1:29:28
12:30	25:00	38:50	50:00	1:02:30	1:17:41	1:33:12
13:00	26:00	40:23	52:00	1:05:00	1:20:47	1:36:58
13:30	27:00	41:57	54:00	1:07:30	1:23:53	1:40:39
14:00	28:00	43:30	56:00	1:10:00	1:27:00	1:43:23

15-K (9.3 mi)	10 mi	20-K (12.43 mi)	Half-marathon (13.1 mi)	15 mi	20 mi	Marathon (26.2 mi)
51:16	55:00	1:08:21	1:12:06	1:22:30	1:50:00	2:24:12
53:36	57:30	1:11:27	1:15:23	1:26:15	1:55:00	2:30:46
55:56	1:00:00	1:14:34	1:18:39	1:30:00	2:00:00	2:37:19
58:15	1:02:30	1:17:40	1:21:56	1:33:45	2:05:00	2:43:52
:00:35	1:05:00	1:20:47	1:25:13	1:37:30	2:10:00	2:50:25
:02:55	1:07:30	1:23:53	1:28:29	1:41:15	2:15:00	2:56:59
:05:15	1:10:00	1:26:59	1:31:46	1:45:00	2:20:00	3:03:32
:07:35	1:12:30	1:30:06	1:35:02	1:48:45	2:25:00	3:10:05
:09:54	1:15:00	1:33:12	1:38:19	1:52:30	2:30:00	3:26:39
1:12:14	1:17:30	1:36:19	1:41:36	1:56:15	2:35:00	3:23:12
1:14:34	1:20:00	1:39:25	1:44:52	2:00:00	2:40:00	3:29:45
1:16:54	1:22:30	1:42:31	1:48:09	2:03:45	2:45:00	3:36:18
1:19:14	1:25:00	1:45:38	1:51:28	2:07:30	2:50:00	3:42:52
1:21:34	1:27:30	1:48:44	1:54:42	2:11:15	2:55:00	3:49:25
1:23:53	1:30:00	1:51:51	1:57:59	2:15:00	3:00:00	3:55:58
1:26:13	1:32:30	1:54:57	2:01:15	2:18:45	3:05:00	4:02:32
1:28:33	1:35:00	1:58:03	2:04:32	2:22:30	3:10:00	4:09:05
1:30:53	1:37:30	2:01:10	2:07:49	2:26:15	3:15:00	4:15:38
1:33:13	1:40:00	2:04:16	2:11:06	2:30:00	3:20:00	4:22:11
1:37:52	1:45:00	2:10:29	2:17:39	2:37:30	3:30:00	4:35:18
1:42:32	1:50:00	2:16:42	2:24:12	2:45:00	3:40:00	4:48:25
1:47:11	1:55:00	2:22:55	2:30:45	2:52:30	3:50:00	5:01:31
1:51:51	2:00:00	2:29:07	2:37:18	3:00:00	4:00:00	5:14:38
1:56:31	2:05:00	2:35:20	2:43:52	3:07:30	4:10:00	5:27:44
2:01:10	2:10:00	2:41:33	2:50:25	3:15:00	4:20:00	5:40:51
2:05:50	2:15:00	2:47:46	2:56:58	3:22:30	4:30:00	5:53:57
2:10:30	2:20:00	2:53:59	3:03:32	3:30:00	4:40:00	6:07:04

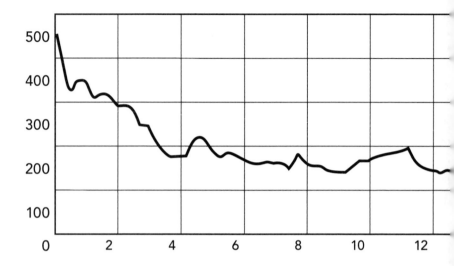

How to Read a Course Elevation Chart

Many races—particularly larger, longer ones—provide course elevation charts or elevation profiles that show how much you will gain or lose in elevation, from start to finish. (The example shown here is the course elevation chart of the Boston Marathon; as the chart shows, this race is a net descent from Hopkinton to Boston.)

Distance is plotted along the X axis; elevation, along the Y. Simple, right? Wrong.

Course elevation charts are nearly always misleading. This is one of road racing's dirty little secrets. The data on such charts may be technically accurate, but they do little to nothing to convey the actual experience of running the actual race.

Using the Boston example: A first-time Boston runner might look at this chart and think to herself, *Wow, look at that. Right from the start, we dive downhill for, like, 15 miles. Then there are a few hills, then a long downhill finish. Awesome!*

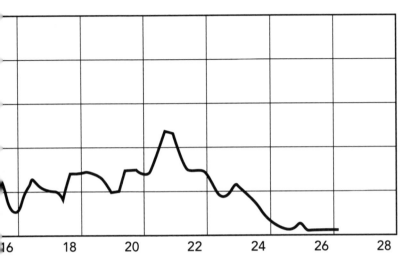

Any Boston Marathon veteran, however, will tell you that the actual race experience is more like this: *OK, little downhill, flat...flat...flat... hill, hill... HILL! OW! WHOA!... MORE HILLS!... I'M DYING!... Oh, finally, there's the finish line...*

So if you want to know how hilly a certain race course is, you should ask someone who's run that race, right?

Wrong again! (Boy, you're terrible at this, aren't you?)

In our experience, first-person accounts of race course elevation are remarkably unreliable. This is because "hilly" is a subjective word. A hilly course for a runner from Kansas may seem "flat as a pancake" to a runner from Colorado.

The *Field Guide*'s advice? If you want a mile-by-mile description of the course of a race, then run, bike, or drive it before race day.

And use course elevation profiles for entertainment purposes only.

Index

Underscored page references indicate boxed text. **Boldface** references indicate illustrations.